Initiation Rites of Young Men and Male Warrior Brotherhoods in Early Germanic Culture

Initiation Rites of Young Men and Male Warrior Brotherhoods in Early Germanic Culture

A Contribution to the Study of Germanic and Nordic Antiquity and Folklore

By Dr. Lily Weiser

Translated by Tom Billinge

Published by Sanctus Arya Press

First edition, published June 2026 by Sanctus Arya Press.

Paperback: 978-1-968394-06-6

Hardcover: 978-1-968394-07-3

Library of Congress number pending.

Editing by Tom Billinge and Benjamin Sieghart.

Layout by Benjamin Sieghart.

Cover art by Tom Billinge.

Inside illustrations taken from the public domain.

More at:

tombillinge.com

sanctusarya.com

An 1872 sketch of a Torslunda plate from Öland, Sweden (c. 6th-8th century) depicting a dancing warrior (or possibly the god Odin) and bear or wolf warrior.

Table of Contents

Translator's Foreword

Initiation Rites of Young Men and Male Warrior Brotherhoods in Early Germanic Culture by Dr Lily Weiser is a forgotten gem of Indo-European studies. Originally published in 1927 as *Altgermanische Jünglingsweihen und Männerbünde: Ein Beitrag zur deutschen und nordischen Altertums- und Volkskunde,* it was the first part of a series called Building Blocks for Folklore and the Study of Religion.

Lily Weiser-Aall was born in Vienna in 1898 to an upper middle-class family. In 1922 her thesis *Jul* (later published as *Jul, Weihnachtsgeschenke und Weihnachtsbaum. Eine volkskundliche Untersuchung ihrer Geschichte*) gained her a PhD at the University of Vienna. Weiser became intimately connected with the folklorists of Europe at that time and with the help of her doctoral advisor Rudolf Much and Eugen Fehrle she wrote *Altgermanische Jünglingsweihen und Männerbünde* which strongly influenced the work of Otto Höfler and English archaeologist Neil Price.

By the outbreak of the Second World War, Weiser was a widowed mother of three. In order to support her family, she begrudgingly took up a post with the German Ahnenerbe at the

Reichsuniversität Straßburg. She had been put in contact with the Ahnenerbe in 1937 by Fehrle, who had been appointed Professor of Classical Philology at the University of Heidelberg.

Weiser never supported the regime and had a serious run-in with the SS upon refusing to collaborate with them. After the War, she and Höfler were able to resume their academic careers, while Fehrle was convicted in 1950 of being a Fellow Traveller and never returned to academia. Weiser became the senior conservator at Norwegian Museum of Cultural History into the 1960s. She died aged 88 in 1987.

Initiation Rites of Young Men and Male Warrior Brotherhoods in Early Germanic Culture is her great contribution to Indo-Germanic folklore and philology. The work pieces together the evidence for the southern and northern Germanic reflexes of the *männerbund* and the initiation of young men into the warrior class. It is a remarkable work that has never been published since its German language version in 1927.

This work sheds light on practices lost to the mists of time through a painstakingly well-researched study of the extant sources from Tacitus to the Germanic sagas, as well as later folklore and fairytale. It paints a vivid and compelling picture of the Germanic *männerbund* tradition and compares it to other Indo-European traditions as well as drawing from more modern tribal initiation rites. It is a pithy and precise work that delivers all of this within a slim volume.

It has been a joy to rediscover what Dr Lily Weiser-Aall brought to light almost a century ago.

Tom Billinge
February 2026

Introduction

The series of publications whose first volume is presented here aims initially to contribute to the development of the still little-clarified field of religious folklore.

The principal domain of folklore is religion. For religious experience in the early stages of cultural development and in the foundational layer of every culture is far more deeply rooted, far more intense, and in its individual manifestations far more varied and vivid than in later stages of development.

Folklore, which investigates such foundational layers, in many respects follows the same paths as the study of religion. The further development of the ideas and forms arising from lived experience it leaves to the history of religion and of culture. Folklore stands in a relationship to both, similar to that of geology to geography. It provides the groundwork for the study of personal culture, often indicates its direction, and shows the interaction between community and personality. Thus, folklore and the study of religion, by clarifying the lower levels and primitive experiences, make an essential contribution to cultural history.

"Only through comparison with the lower forms of religion does the essential nature of the higher become fully clear, and only in the struggle of the religious genius to free itself from these primitive beginnings and ever strive to create something new can the meaning of religion in its fulfilment be revealed" (Hauer, *Die Religionen*, I, p. VI). In such comparisons, the aim is less to collect the survivals of past times and worldviews for antiquarian reasons than to perceive the divine power that is eternal and continually leads humanity back to the same primal experiences.

I call these booklets "Building Blocks." They are intended to present treatises and source works for folklore and the study of religion. This does not mean that every volume must belong to both fields; works will also be included that concern only one or the other.

The present first volume by Dr. Lily Weiser investigates the question of whether and to what extent the youth initiations and men's leagues found across the world were known among the Germanic peoples.

In order to recognise the remnants preserved in Germanic traditions, the psychological and religious foundations of the initiations and leagues, their forms, and their processes of decline are first presented as they appear among so-called "primitive" peoples. The core of initiation is the period of transition and instruction in which the young people enter into the closest relationship with the gods of the tribe and are trained to become members of the community. Following this foundation, the second section discusses the reports concerning the Chatti, Harii, Heruli, and Taifali. It becomes evident that the ancient Germanic peoples also possessed men's leagues and a fully developed youth initiation. Their nature is described in detail from the rich Norse tradition. At the centre of the discussion stand the Norse berserkers. Of great importance is the thorough examination of the individual initiation rites.

The overall phenomenon dates back to Indo-Germanic (Indo-European) times. Many features, for example traces of totemism, point to a very great antiquity. By the time of the written sources, the leagues had developed into clearly defined warrior bands. This transformation appears to have gone hand-in-hand with the introduction of and merging with the cult of Wodan. The connection of the warrior bands with older religious leagues is evident in the league of the Chatti, the Harii, the berserkers, and the Lombardic Cynocephali.

The principal viewpoints that emerged from the consideration of religious foundational experiences are clearly worked out for Germanic antiquity; however, the Germanic material is treated entirely within Germanic cultural conditions. Thus, methodologically, a proper balance is maintained between comparative and historical folklore. A number of phenomena and literary traditions have been placed into new and important contexts. In this way, many individual questions of the study of antiquity and folklore have been illuminated and advanced on the basis of a large body of material.

The publisher, who alongside the newly founded *Uberdeutschen Zeitschrift für Volkskunde* has also undertaken these "Building Blocks," deserves heartfelt thanks for his understanding support and his promotion of our scholarship.

Heidelberg
Eugen Fehrle

The editor, Professor Dr. Eugen Fehrle, with proven helpfulness made the rapid printing possible and furthered my work through valuable advice and suggestions. I would also like to express my sincere thanks to him here. I owe much support to Professor Much. To him, to Professor R. Hoffmann, and to my father I am grateful for the painstaking review of the proofs.

Vienna, January 1927
Lily Weiser

State of Research and Research Question

In attempting to investigate and understand the historical development of individual Christmas customs, it became apparent, first, that only a very small part of these traditions is tied exclusively to the Christmas festival; second, that essential components, when the main customs — especially the various Christmas processions — are analysed, must remain unexplained if interpreted solely in terms of ancestor cult or fertility magic. These elements are characteristic neither of Christmas nor of other annual festivals, and yet they recur throughout Europe at major festival times from ancient days onward.

Very often children, young men, or guilds are the bearers of the customs in question. Their simultaneous occurrence at weddings, at deposition from office, at the admission of journeymen, and the striking comparison with initiation customs (*initium* = beginning) of so-called "primitive" peoples suggested the assumption that they originally belonged to a specific group of rites connected with transitions from one stage of life or social group to another — that is, they may have been initiation rites. The next question was whether such rites of initiation might stem from Germanic antiquity, or whether they were borrowed from classical antiquity, or perhaps were more recent innovations.

For the Indo-Europeans, age classes, associations, and initiation rites have generally been acknowledged (Hirt, Feist). However, the great gap that exists between the 1st century — since certain reports in Tacitus (*Germania*) were interpreted as traces of age classes and initiations — and the 15th century in German tradition has rightly given rise to doubts. Hirt (*Indogermanen* II, p. 252 ff.) allows the assumption of such institutions for the Indo-Europeans but adds:

"This phenomenon exists essentially at lower cultural levels and is largely overcome among European peoples, although remnants and even new formations can probably be demonstrated. The sympathy and bond among those of the same age is such an obvious feature that we must be very careful not to see remnants of ancient times in modern occurrences." The Greek and Roman youth associations recall the youth leagues of the German Middle Ages; "but whether they go back to antiquity cannot be decided."

For the Germanic peoples, more detailed and extensive investigations are lacking. Kaufmann pointed this out in his work on Old Germanic associations. In his *German Antiquities* he gave several indications relevant to this question. The significance of chapter 31 of the *Germania* for youth initiation was suggested by N. E. Hammarstedt in his Swedish translation of Tacitus.

Above all, these indications, along with others mentioned in the second chapter, suggest that much more could still be discovered.

The present study, therefore, if it was to serve the questions indicated, had to take as its task the investigation of that aforementioned gap — the Old Germanic period. "Old Germanic," according to Heusler (*Altgermanische Dichtung*, p. 6), is a cultural concept without strict chronological boundaries: "that Germanic world not precisely defined by Church and classical learning, traces of which reach deep into the Middle Ages."

Guiding for me were the works of my esteemed teacher Rudolf Much and those of Axel Olrik.

The nature of the literary sources for Germanic antiquity — Tacitus and the Old Norse sagas — entails that one cannot proceed by philological-historical method alone. We are dealing with matters that had already largely been overcome by the time these accounts were written and were therefore no longer fully understood even then.

The investigation therefore turns, especially in the Nordic sphere, to those components of ancient tradition that Heusler designates as narrative material — *Erzählstoff, Märchen, Volkssagen, Mythen, Anekdoten* (p. 948). It is precisely this narrative material that comes strongly to the fore in a later period, from the 12th to the 14th centuries (ibid., p. 943).

The motifs of this old narrative material are usually described simply as products of imagination.

I believe, however, that they are in large part rooted in real — specifically religious — life. Religious feeling changes, but the forms remain. From them we can now only rarely sense the original experience, and thus those strange motifs appear to us as products of fantasy — of a love of storytelling. I arrived at this supposition through a small study of Germanic household spirits. This assumption, which starting from so small a point of departure could not be considered firmly established, was deepened, broadened, and raised to conviction through Hauer's work *Die Religionen: ihr Werden, ihr Sinn, ihre Wahrheit.*

Something similar, and very important for the significance of this tradition, was recently stated by Sydow in a study of the fairy tale:

"The fairy tale, as deliberate poetic creation, was able to preserve ancient primitive ideas and customs better than any other literary form. Even when such ideas have completely disappeared from living

popular belief, the fairy tale can preserve them unchanged, because it is permitted to deviate from known reality and therefore old belief motifs can remain unchanged as poetic motifs."

In order to approach the lived experience underlying the phenomena to be examined and thereby recognise the forms in which it becomes visible, the study begins — on a folkloristic basis — with a discussion of the entire institution, which is widespread and surrounded by a series of recurring customs found everywhere.

I

Youth Initiations and Männerbünde Among Tribal Peoples

The first section is intended to describe, in general terms, the nature and the outer and inner development of initiation — insofar as anything definite can be said about it today — and to provide the broad foundation for investigation and questioning with regard to the Old Germanic period.

A self-evident prerequisite for everything that follows is the fact that the word "primitive" is used only in a relative sense. For even in the earliest times and at the lowest cultural levels known to us, higher and lower elements exist side by side or are interwoven with one another. Truly primitive religion or custom is, in fact, not known at all.

The best-known and most important initiation is the youth

initiation, which can be demonstrated — admittedly often only in remnants — among almost all peoples. Today, and already at the time of the older reports on the various peoples, the stage of development of youth initiation is very uneven. If, in what follows, youth initiation is to be sketched in its principal manifestations, then a particular stage of development of the overall phenomenon must serve as the basis.

Naturally, such an overview presupposes a uniform development among all peoples — an assumption that today one is no longer inclined to accept. The task of the first chapter is therefore, in general, to instruct about the nature of the initiation of beginnings and, in doing so, to grasp and draw attention more to the difficulties and questions posed by the material than to attempt to resolve these difficulties through individual investigations. Thus, beyond the manifold actual and inferable forms of development, an average cross-section of the phenomenon must be considered in order to come closer to its core.

The basis of this overview is a condition known from reports about various peoples, which Webster describes as the flowering period of youth initiation. Every youth must undergo the initiation in order to become a man. The tribe therefore consists of all initiated men, and authority lies in the hands of the elders.

For this reason, this youth initiation is often also called a tribal initiation. Its importance for so-called primitive life can hardly be overestimated and has repeatedly been emphasised by researchers.

Initiation is, in fact, the period of schooling of tribal peoples, in which strict discipline and obedience toward superiors are inculcated. Through initiation the youth is introduced into the religious and political tradition of his tribe.

Those who are initiated receive instruction in the necessary skills: hunting, fishing, housebuilding, the manufacture of tools, and so forth. Through initiation they acquire the right and the duty to bear arms, to take part in war, to defend the land, to found a family, to practice the religion and customs, and to pass them on to the next generation.

The uninitiated (W., p. 25 ff.) have no rights, are universally despised, and are beaten by women and children. There are comparatively very few uninitiated persons. In part, they are removed from the world as useless cowards.

In broad outline, puberty initiations proceed as follows:

The boys are summoned to the initiation by those already initiated, usually by their fathers or by the elders of the tribe; at times they are violently torn away from their mothers. The leaders of the initiations are older men or priests, assisted by younger initiates. Often each candidate is assigned a teacher and helper: a "godfather."

The initiations do not take place every year, but rather as needed, at intervals ranging from one to seven years.

As the setting for the solemn rite, a remote place is chosen, which is protected from the intrusion of the uninitiated by numerous measures. Almost everywhere, women and girls are forbidden, under penalty of death, to enter the sacred site.

At this place the young people are completely isolated. The duration of this isolation varies and ranges from several months to several years. The youths must then undergo prolonged trials: fasting, sleep deprivation, poisoning, neglect of the body, not washing, letting the hair grow, dancing to the point of exhaustion, fumigation, and all manner of painful interventions, the most important of which is circumcision.

They are then allegedly devoured by a monster in order to be reborn, or their death and resurrection are symbolically represented in some other way. Often, through the preparations, they actually fall into a death-like state. Frequently the youths are "made into spirits" by being painted with spirit colours, by masks, and by the production of spirit voices.

Of importance is the learning of cult dances and instruction in the religious and moral tradition, as well as seeing and becoming acquainted with the sacred objects of the tribe. Often a secret language is learned.

During the period of isolation, the candidates are sometimes permitted, without punishment, to plunder their surroundings and commit all manner of mischief.

After the end of the "bush period," the initiates return and have completely forgotten their former life. This often goes so far that they must relearn the most ordinary activities, such as walking and eating; they also very frequently receive a new name. The initiation concludes with a general tribal festival, including a ceremonial feast and performances of masked dances. At times, unrestrained orgiastic celebrations are held.

Those initiated at the same time are regarded as being bound together by particularly close ties; often a bond of blood-brotherhood is also ritually established between the newly initiated and the elders or fathers.

The initiates are no longer subject to their mothers, and it is strictly forbidden for them to play with children. Often all instruments and objects used in the initiation are burned.

When one takes a general, necessarily cursory overview of the initiation of youths — which naturally cannot do justice to the extremely diverse forms found among individual peoples — one gains the immediate impression that this is a complex of rites that has undergone a long and intricate process of development. What we have before us today derives from various stages of religious and social evolution; it is to a great extent already socially emphasised, systematised, and rationalised. Nevertheless, the religious foundation remains recognisable even in the most degenerate remnants.

The great difficulty faced by all attempts at explanation, arising from the obscurity of the historical development of initiation customs, has repeatedly been emphasised. It is therefore likely that any explanation will remain deficient and incomplete if it seeks to derive the entire complex from a single cause or to "explain" the customs and beliefs of so-called primitive peoples according to the logical laws of modern thought. An interpretation can only be adequate if it proceeds from the pre-logical and mystical state of mind of primitive peoples (Lévy-Bruhl, *passim*). Given our insufficient knowledge of so-called primitive peoples, it will scarcely be possible to reconstruct and fully comprehend their primal feelings and experiences. One must therefore content oneself with uncovering the principal components.

The most important earlier attempts to explain youth initiations have recently been clearly compiled and discussed by Dr. Moritz Zeller; since I am not concerned here with individual details of primitive initiation, I may refer to his work. All these explanations (p. 159) fail to satisfy. Zeller himself is, on the whole, provisionally in agreement with the explanation offered by psychoanalysis (especially Reik), but he emphasises in particular that the religious element was originally the principal component of the boys' initiation (p. 160). This is very important and has been repeatedly suggested in earlier explanatory attempts, but it has never been fully grasped or properly appreciated — even by Zeller, who strives for psychological depth.

It is regrettable that Zeller was unfamiliar with Gennep's work *Les rites de passage*, in which a fundamentally new psychological approach to initiation rites was established. Gennep departs from questions of origin and function and directs attention to the core of the experience itself: the idea of transformation, of rebirth, which places the novice into a new world.

According to Gennep, initiation rites belong as a subdivision to the "rites de passage." Such rites of transition play a major role in all important transitions in human life, above all at birth, marriage, and death; at the arrival of a stranger; in housebuilding; and upon entry into a specific, clearly delimited sphere of life or society. According to Gennep, they consist of three main parts:

1 rites of separation (*séparation*) from the previous environment;
2 rites of a transitional or liminal period (*marge*);
3 rites of incorporation or attachment to the new environment (*agrégation*) (Chapter I).

Above all, the intermediate or transitional period is of the greatest significance. It is a state that is, as it were, legally and morally unprotected, suspended between two worlds: alienated from the familiar, not yet incorporated into the foreign, and exposed to the influence of mysterious powers. It is in every respect an exceptional condition. This state is such an essential experiential fact of every initiation that it requires closer examination.

Anyone who has personally undergone a significant transition in life has experienced a stronger or weaker sense of this exceptional state. Certain beliefs connected with such times have also been preserved among so-called educated people — for example, before a wedding, a first journey, a major undertaking, a first public appearance, or an examination. Even today, this exceptional condition is not only felt by the person concerned but is often also recognised and respected by others.

In folk belief, transitional periods are known to play the greatest role. These include the days before major festivals, especially the Twelve Nights, during which the otherworld stands open and demonic powers freely pursue their activity; the time of pregnancy; the period between birth and baptism; between betrothal and marriage; to a great extent the period between death and burial, followed by the mourning period. The ancient and ever-renewed experience underlying these ideas found its highest artistic expression in Schiller's *Wallenstein* (*Wallenstein's Death*, Act II, Scene 3):

"There exist moments in the life of man, when he is nearer the great Soul of the world than is man's custom, and possesses freely the power of questioning his destiny."

But not only times, also specific places evoke such feelings, both in popular belief and in the child's imagination. Boundaries, crossroads, doors, bridges, and the like are perceived as uncanny and dangerous places — locations where all manner of invisible forces carry out their play. Künßberg emphasizes in *Rechtsbrauch und Kinderspiel* (p. 12) that in the child's psyche there exists a sacred dread of boundaries.

"The line that separates the homely, familiar, one's own, from the unknown is crossed with a certain superstitious tension and a sense of adventure." Certainly, this is not a feeling related to the legal significance of the boundary, although children often have a keen sense of their own sphere of rights.

Nor do I believe that, in folk legends of boundary violators who must wander after death, only the ethically motivated and later idea of punishment and atonement (Boette, p. 50) is decisive. Rather, this appears merely as a subsequent rationalisation of the ancient dread of boundaries that comes to the foreground. Whoever crosses the boundary places themselves in danger; whoever violates it falls prey to demonic powers.

Frequently, the two notions — spatial and temporal — merge and mutually reinforce one another; again and again in magical practices and festivals one hears the formula: *"at a specific time, in a specific place."*

A general conception of important transitions and beginnings, and the expression of this conception through actions, asserts itself already in the lives of the simplest peoples; it presupposes merely a distinction between the ordinary and the extraordinary. According to Wundt, it is above all catastrophic events that first make an impression on human beings; the regular and routine is noticed only later. Thus, rites first arise in connection with the most significant transitions, such as birth and death, and their reenactment or symbols are repeatedly used to represent other transitions as well. From this perspective one can also explain, for example, the frequent close connection between the cult of the dead and initiation rites.

The tripartite structure of all rites, as described by Gennep, is particularly clear in the initiation of youths:

1 rites of separation, the removal from home and from the mother;
2 the transitional period (*marge*), which is especially favourable for contact with the other world at a consecrated place (spirit-place);
3 incorporation into the new world and return to everyday life, which likely begins already with instruction in

everyday skills and reaches its climax in the communal feast.

What is important and new in Gennep's conception is the recognition that there are periods in human life that are especially suited to religious experiences and inner transformations. The rites of passage have their deepest foundation in experiences that bring about such transitions in the human soul — and not only in that of so-called primitive peoples. Sauer (pp. 27–46) raises the question of what primitive religious experiences are like.

The core of these experiences is of an ecstatic nature: a being touched or seized by a superhuman power that is experienced as the highest reality. Within the experience, the certainty of truth is given immediately; this experience is so powerful that it signifies the beginning of a new life process, a turning point in one's life.

That such a fundamental experience can vary greatly among different peoples and individuals is obvious. Among peoples with a strong disposition toward ecstasy, such as the North American Indians, ecstasy — which in itself is already understood as initiation, for example among the Crow — therefore comes strongly to the fore. Among other peoples, by contrast, preparation for the ecstatic experience plays the principal role; this will become clear from the examples.

Opposed to the natural, primarily physically conditioned transitions — birth, puberty, death — stand primarily psychologically conditioned, extraordinary experiences and self-willed resolutions. Yet even in this contrast one senses how intimately the two are connected.

The nature of both types of initiation experiences is most easily grasped by examining primitive priests and magicians, where the bodily conditioning of such experiences also clearly emerges from various indications. This is very important, because in this way the many cruelties of initiation rites, which offend our sensibilities, can nevertheless be recognised as religious acts — admittedly of a kind foreign and coarse to us.

Among most peoples there are individual persons to whom spirits reveal themselves and who claim to recognise secret powers, to disarm them, and to rule over them: these are the magicians. Their ability rests on natural disposition, on a predisposition to strong ecstatic experiences. In very early times this gift — like madness — appears as "holy," whereas later periods tend to regard it as "pathological," probably also because such people are often physically weak and sickly. Well known are the states of the Lappish and Siberian shamans. But the situation is no different in the Germanic world. The Old Norse word *skratte* ("magician"), for example, expresses this as well; it belongs to a word group whose basic meaning is "to be sickly," "to be weak." (Falk–Torp, *skrante*.)

In Germanic regions, there are people in Scotland, Norway, and Germany who are believed to be endowed with a "second sight." They are described as pale, earnest, shy, tormented individuals (cf., for example, Jonas Lie, *The Seer*; Droste-Hülshoff, *Westphalian Sketches*; Justinus Kerner). Particularly well known are the *Spöken- oder Schichtrieker* of Westphalia (Gartori, p. 75f.). This gift is almost always innate, but it can also be transmitted when someone steps on the right foot of the afflicted person and looks over the left shoulder.

This conception within our own people is of great significance, for it contains the fundamental ideas of magical-religious initiation. Magical power — that is, the capacity for states of heightened excitation and extraordinary states of the soul, for visions and hallucinations — rests on disposition. Yet experience had to teach that this capacity belongs, to some degree, to many, indeed almost all, people, but that in most cases it manifests itself only under particular conditions, for example in states of intoxication or weakness. In cases of need, such conditions were therefore deliberately produced. In the case just mentioned, this occurs in a very diluted form through a casual act of transmission.

Thus, alongside the calling in which the spirit unexpectedly comes over a person, there early appear forms brought about through specific ceremonies and through training, although ecstatic disposition always remains a prerequisite (Sauer, 462). The more artificial such training becomes, however, the more worthless the experiences ultimately are, until they often end in outright deception — though this says nothing against the authenticity of the phenomenon as a whole. With Sauer (449), one must adopt the principle: *"First the experience, then the imitation,"* as the basis of interpretation.

It is striking how even today the German people distinguish between those who, by virtue of their disposition, are seers and healers, and those who push themselves toward the spirit world through conjuration. The former are respected and pitied; the latter are shunned (Boette, 80–97). In this view, conscious feeling gives the decisive impulse, but fundamentally the evaluation rests on the distinction between the "genuine" and the "inauthentic." What becomes clear is the gradual substitution of artificial assistance for the original calling, a process that ultimately leads to a reversal of the basic relationship, as can be seen when considering Siberian customs. *"True, ancient shamanism,"* writes T. Lehtisalo in *Entwurf einer Mythologie Der Jurak-Smojeden* (p. 144), *"rests upon a pathological endowment that, according to popular belief, is inherited and manifests itself sooner or later, usually already in early youth."*

Occasionally one can recognise at birth that a child will become a shaman (p. 146). If a child is born wearing a shirt that covers the entire body, he will become the greatest magician; the least powerful is one whose head alone is covered at birth. The future magician has visions, sings in his sleep, and when spending the night in the forest, spirits come to him and urge him to summon them for help in cases of illness. At the age of twenty, the adept enters into apprenticeship with an old magician. The magician Raikka related in Obdorsk that the old magician first taught his pupil, at a sacred site during the day, the singing of magic songs and the beating of his drum. Then he makes a drum for the young shaman himself. When the younger man's own drum is finished, they go in the evening, fasting, to the sacred place, where the magician beats the drum while the younger man initially merely assists. When he himself begins to drum (p. 147), human-shaped spirits first come to him in great numbers. He becomes agitated, and the old magician leaves him there overnight. After spending the night in intercourse with the spirits, who give him final instruction as a magician, he returns home at daybreak.

From that point on, he is a shaman without special rites. Had the spirits been hostile to him during the night, he would have remained dead on the spot. In roughly the same way, a Lapp becomes a shaman: he is visited by spirits and goes into training with an experienced magician. In *Sibirsky Vestnik* (1822), it is reported of the Tungus: "*He who wishes to become a shaman reports that such-and-such a deceased shaman appeared to him in his sleep and commanded him to become a shaman.*"

Actual initiation rites in Siberia exist only among the Buryats, when someone wishes to become a white shaman. (Yet these rites are, as Holmberg has shown in *der Baum des Lebens*, pp. 141ff., borrowed cultural material.) The black shamans — that is, those who associate with subterranean spirits — have no noteworthy rites, except that they dare to remain at night at the sacred place where such spirits dwell and to offer them sacrifices.

I would nevertheless like to regard all these reports as forms of initiation. What is original is that anyone to whom spirits appear can become a shaman. The vision alone already counts as initiation. If shamanism is understood as hereditary, this already implies an individualisation and the beginning of a forming professional class, and sometimes the natural endowment must be artificially assisted: a lonely sacred place is sought out. Even the instrument of the shaman's estate, the drum, is "handed over" and thus constitutes a fairly substantial initiation.

The development into a professional class is further promoted by the training that the novice receives from a professional magician. Much more highly developed and more self-conscious is the other type of Siberian initiation. Its principal content is the journey of the shaman into heaven, which is illustrated and actually carried out.

The totality of these rites strikingly recalls the initiations of the Mithras mysteries and other Oriental conceptions. The details, as well as the idea of the soul's journey in general, are not based on the original religious conceptions of the Turko-Tatar peoples.

The difference between the two kinds of initiation rests on the reversal of the relationship of the novice to the other world. In the first process, the person concerned is visited by spirits, thus chosen by them; in the second, however, the adept visits the spirits and in doing so employs means determined by tradition and proven effective by experience. He is no longer called, but compels and masters the other world, from which he returns knowingly and enlightened. In other words, we are dealing with two consecrations that stand on entirely different stages of development. In the first type, religious endowment alone decides; in the second, religious technique predominates. Numerous examples of primitive prophetic initiation are reported by Sauer (index under "prophetic initiation"). The more highly developed forms are largely shaped after the model of youth initiations and have in turn influenced these again.

At this point I have treated the calling and consecration of magicians somewhat more extensively, because from them the religious purpose of the torments of youth initiations becomes especially clear. All these means — fasting, sleeplessness, fumigation, poisonings, not washing, beatings, movement to the point of exhaustion, thus ultimately all kinds of dances, solitude and seclusion — are intended to lead to the preparation and awakening of powerful religious impressions and, for the central moment of the initiation, the transformation, assimilation, or intercourse with the other world, to open the soul. In other words, through these preparations the waking consciousness is to be emptied for extraordinary processes arising from the unconscious; ultimately, ecstasy is to be produced. That in these measures other feelings and drives have also cooperated in a creative and formative way is clear. For example, many of them aim at thorough bodily purification, while others simultaneously represent tests of courage and strength. This again shows how complex the psychological foundations of these rites are.

The central point of initiation, however, is the entering into connection with the other world, and this has been understood by all researchers as religious in nature. Frobenius in particular has clearly demonstrated for Africa the intimate connection between initiation and ancestor worship (*Masken und Geheimbünde* passim; cf. Lévy-Bruhl p. 317).

Very often this penetration into the spirit realm and union with the other world is represented as death and rebirth. Why precisely the image of death and birth is so frequently chosen for establishing connection with superhuman powers is understandable for many reasons. It has already been emphasised that both are archetypal images of transition. Death as absolute cessation of life is incomprehensible to primitive peoples; for them it is a "becoming-other," a transition into another world, that of the spirits of the dead and demons. Even this conception may rest on experiential facts. Besides simple dreams and visions, the most impressive experience is the death-like sleep of the enraptured person and the sudden falling asleep known as catalepsy (especially frequent in African initiations), followed by awakening and recounting the experiences. Such a state — particularly when it lasted a long time — may well have been regarded as actual death, and when people with weaker cataleptic disposition were to be made into magicians, they were symbolically killed or weakened until they entered a similar condition. For the whole rite is not concerned with an intellectual grasp or conceptual linking of death and rebirth, but with an emotional clarification of powerful religious impressions. It is also of the greatest importance that primitive peoples, and indeed our own as well, as Dieterich emphasises, are not able to conceive a developmental process, but tend to understand gradual development as a sudden event, usually under the image of death and rebirth (p. 157). Thus, a human being does not develop from boy to youth; rather, the boy dies and the youth is born.

There is, however, yet another way to achieve that penetration into the spirit world, that transcendence beyond everyday life: through masks or what is equivalent to them, the painting or transformation of the body. The wearer of a mask is completely identical with the demon or animal he represents. He himself is wholly convinced of it; he is practically "possessed," and the spectators too believe unreservedly in the unity of performer and represented being. The latter can also be observed in children: they fear masks even when they know who is behind them. How serious this belief was among peoples at an early cultural stage is shown also by the fact that masks, when not in use, were kept as sacred objects. It is further instructive that in New Guinea it was forbidden under penalty of death for the uninitiated to attempt to recognise the bearer of a mask as a person (W. 101).

On the other hand, as mentioned, the mask also acts suggestively upon the wearer himself. I refer here especially to the numerous examples of animal possession given by Sauer. Particularly vivid is the following report in Horneffer I, p. 177: a traveller unexpectedly pulled a bear glove over a shaman's hand. Horrified, he stared at the altered hand, began to growl and move like a bear, and calmed down only after the glove was removed.

All the forms of expression of the primitive longing for the spirit world mentioned above may occur together in initiations or each separately. Alongside the religious fundamental experiences discussed and their most important modes of expression, however, there is still another fact accompanying all initiations that is of greater significance: the different initiations confer not only religious elevation but also social rights.

At least as important as birth and death for peoples of lower cultural level is the transition of puberty. Therefore Sauer (p. 430) rightly calls the initiation of youths "the primeval central act of the tribe." It serves as a model for other initiations and in turn receives expansions from experiences in other spheres (cf. p. 20). If the youth initiation lasts a longer time, several years, it often ends with marriage, or a stage of bachelorhood is inserted between youth and manhood initiations. The three stages — childhood, manhood, old age — are the natural age classes (Wundt, *Völkerpsychologie* VII, p. 324 ff.). They form groups which, unlike the family, sex, and tribe based on blood relationship, may already be called social. Thus, wherever we encounter youth initiation, social development is already at a fairly high level. This initiation is no longer purely religious; it already confers social rights and privileges. How, then, did the development from religious experience to social institution take place? Here lies the great difficulty, and this question has not yet been satisfactorily answered.

Behind the tribal initiations there is also concealed the struggle between two generations (cf. note 18), as well as the struggle for male dominance over women. The initiation of women sometimes takes place simultaneously with that of men, but on the whole it appears to be less public. It is not, as Schurtz assumes, always merely a weak imitation of male initiations. Schurtz arrives at this view because he explains the age-classes together with initiations solely from the instinctive urge toward sociability, which in his opinion is much less developed in women than in men.

According to Webster (45), the initiation of women is less important because it brings with it fewer privileges. Both of these views must be judged as products of the scholars' one-sidedly social standpoint and can be justified only from that perspective. The social initiation of women is closely connected with their position in the primitive state, where, however, they are usually rather suppressed. But if one takes into account the profound religious significance of initiations and rites of passage, it becomes clear that the initiation of women is also of great importance, even if it is naturally shaped differently than that of men. For the most part, the initiation rites of women seem to be attached to marriage, which is all the more probable since, in the known initiations of girls, marriage immediately follows.

Alongside tribal initiation, *männerbünde* (men's associations) — especially the secret societies — possess entrance initiations. The fundamental significance of these societies is, as Hauer (421 ff.) has shown, religious. Their ultimate origin is unclear. The account that Hauer gives of their presumed development is likewise unclear. At the beginning of his investigation (p. 479), he regards the initiation of youths as the *"first form of a shared religious experience based on instruction in the sacred tradition of the tribe."*

On p. 483 he presents the age-classes, which Wundt considers the natural foundation of youth initiations, as offshoots of the societies under the influence of social and political instincts. Wundt (*Völkerpsychologie* VII, 1, 330) calls it a reversal of the natural sequence of phenomena if one derives the age-classes only from cult associations. The age-classes seem in any case to be a far more general phenomenon than the societies; they are given by nature itself, whereas the development of the societies depends on various external conditions (cf. Wundt, loc. cit., p. 322).

With the initiation of youths, it should be emphasised once more, the cult of ancestors and of the dead is frequently closely connected, and with it all those magical rites intended to promote rain, sunshine, and growth. The close relationship between the veneration of the dead and vegetation rites is well known.

According to Webster, the flourishing period of tribal initiation lasts as long as the leadership of the tribe remains in the hands of the elders. The tribe then consists of all initiated men, divided into the classes of bachelors, married men, and elders, and thus forms as a whole a society whose grades each person can attain only through various ceremonies kept secret from the uninitiated, from women, and naturally from strangers to the tribe.

This is, as noted above, the stage of development that underlies the general outline of youth initiation. With the growth of population, with increasing agriculture, and especially when authority passes from the hands of the elders into those of a single leader, this institution no longer suffices. In Chapter VIII Webster has described a series of different phenomena of decline or transformation, some of which must be mentioned.

In part, when a leader raises himself above the tribe, secret societies arise out of the age-classes; or the leader appropriates the youth initiation and from this there develops the foundation for a kind of following, as for example among South African tribes (W. 80). Some of the secret societies retain their earlier democratic character in that all young men must pass through their lower grades. The societies often develop either into religious brotherhoods, social clubs, or professional associations. Wundt (p. 330) interprets this development as a one-sided elaboration of motives (religious and social) that in primitive tribal initiation are united. Yet alongside this one must, with Hauer (485), regard the societies as religious central phenomena rather than secondary ones. Precisely such ancient societies often hold the youth initiation in their hands.

One sign of decline is the appearance of several secret societies with special purposes, with a kind of division of labor. Degeneration into robber societies can also be observed. Secret societies frequently practice deliberate deception. In some places the decline seems to have begun even before the intrusion of Europeans; Christianity has usually accelerated it greatly.

A sure sign of the decay of the old tribal initiation is the admission of members of every age, of women, and finally of outsiders. Yet among peoples highly gifted in religion this very development also signifies a great inner advance: in contrast to the external community of tribe or custom, spiritual kinship stands as the binding power of the association (cf. Hauer 458).

This is the case with the highly developed North American brotherhoods (Midewiwin), which vividly recall the ancient mysteries.

A quite different development is taken by the associations of this type in Africa, in which the religious element almost entirely disappears and the social element appears strongly developed. Here a kind of police and tribunal arises.

The latter two kinds of associations have completely lost their connection with the old youth initiation, but their rites of consecration are still essentially the same as in the youth initiation. The last remnants of tribal initiations and of the secret societies often present themselves as entertainment clubs. Yet even there, as Hauer has shown, the religious substratum almost always still glimmers through.

Alongside these lines of development there arise at all times societies that are called forth by special events, such as epidemics and other disasters, which either help new ideas to victory or wish to preserve the old, and which are organised according to the pattern of already existing associations.

For the following investigation it is important to learn something also about the decline and degeneration of the individual initiation rites. In part they disappear entirely. Among the western tribes of Victoria in Australia, the young man must spend a period (12 months) far away from his home.

When he then returns home to take part in the first great tribal assembly, all his beard hairs are plucked out and he must drink a disgusting potion (W. 78). In another tribe the youths are shaved, their heads covered with clay, then their bodies smeared with filth, and thus they must remain outdoors for several days and nights and throw dirt at everyone they see.

The Manga ceremonies of the Fijians have lost all severity and the novices no longer have to endure either trials or purifications during their conclusion. Circumcision too is no longer practiced here in connection with initiation, but on special occasions, for example in the illness of an important person. It is also significant that initiation no longer necessarily has to precede marriage.

In general the decay of the rites shows itself in the fact that they are no longer secret, no longer so strict and harsh (W. 79). In part the youth initiation is replaced by a festival at which the adolescents receive a gift. Often the youth initiation is understood no longer as admission into the class of men, but into childhood prolonged.

Masks too are then often no longer regarded as sacred, and the men who once performed holy dances go through the village with lanterns and the ringing of bells in order to collect money and food for the festival (among the Aymara, Bolivia, W. 177). The villagers still regard them with reverence, and mothers frighten their undressed children with them. But matters can go so far that sacred instruments, above all the widely distributed *Schwirrholz* (bullroarer), sink to the level of children's toys.

The survey of the decline of initiation shows the following: first, the youth initiation loses its political significance for the community and can disappear entirely. The psychic forces that produced it remain in existence: the religious experience of transition and the struggle of two generations. All later phenomena may at first be new formations without historical connection, for the psychological foundations are strong enough at any time to create new associations out of themselves.

On closer inspection, however, this refers chiefly to the legal form and the social significance of the matter. One must reckon with a comparatively rapid development of legal institutions, often brought about by external causes. It has already been mentioned that associations can form through extraordinary events (epidemics, political upheavals).

Precisely in the one-sided further development of the legal-social side the religious significance fades overall. It seems different, however, with the individual rites and usages of the new formations; there one readily has recourse to inherited tradition. But since the transitional periods in the life of each individual, regardless of what development state life takes, remain the same, the customs connected with them are also preserved alive among the people through manifold transmission.

That such an overview of the initiation of the primitive peoples is possible at all clearly shows how similar in structure and nature the phenomenon is over a wide area. Especially important, to emphasise once more, is the transitional or intermediate period in which religious excitations, trials, and instruction place the initiands into an exceptional state. This becomes outwardly visible through seclusion, costume, masks, and above all through special liberties — the right of the candidates to plunder, rob, even to kill.

II

Old Germanic Youth Initiations and Männerbünde

Proceeding from the experience and the psychological foundations of rites of passage and initiations, the question must be answered in the affirmative: Did the ancient Germans also possess an initiation and, connected with it, cultic associations? This can be affirmed, at least in general, especially with reference to the reports of Tacitus in the *Germania* and to the surviving remnants found in later folk custom. For a general overview I refer to Haberlandt. In summary one may say: for Europe the age-class of the youths or bachelors is particularly clearly discernible, as well as the associations of the closed body of young men. *"Through the brotherhoods of young men three forms of the social existence of youth appear regulated: love life, military activity, and finally the cultic connection with the ancient powers of nature..."* (Haberlandt, p. 611)

But how this institution was constituted in Old Germanic times has not yet been treated in broader scope. The following investigation attempts to contribute to its solution.

First, I shall give a brief overview of the most important Indian, Greek, and Roman initiation rites.

In the *Gṛhyasūtras*, the descriptions of domestic usages, the initiation or girding ceremony (*Upanayana*) is described in detail. Since this solemnity is not mentioned in the *Ṛgveda*, one might suspect it to be an innovation; yet this assumption is refuted by ethnological parallels.

Oldenberg (*Religion des Veda*, p. 466 ff.) considers the *Upanayana* ceremony — something long since recognised by ethnology — to be the *"Vedic form of the ancient youth initiation"* (p. 468). The principal features of the *Upanayana*, the introduction to the teacher — primitive initiation as a whole may in fact be regarded as a school — are as follows. The boy is fed, shaved, adorned, and receives a new garment that has not yet been washed.

Then the sacrificial fire is solemnly kindled and the necessary implements are brought forth: a stone, a garment not yet washed, an antelope skin, a threefold girdle, and so forth. A fire-offering by the teacher follows.

The boy must step with his right foot upon the stone while a formula is recited, in which he is exhorted to be firm like the stone. With the appropriate recitations the new garment, the girdle, and the antelope skin are placed upon him.

The boy now asks for initiation; the teacher inquires after the pupil's name, takes his hand, and through various symbolic touches indicates that he takes possession of him, and imparts to him instruction concerning his future duties. The pupil for the first time tends the fire, receives a staff, and must go begging. A three-day fast follows. The duties of the pupil consist in tending the fire, begging, sleeping on the ground, and obedience toward the teacher. After completion of the course of instruction, during which chastity must be observed and which lasts until the pupil has learned the *Veda*, a concluding feast takes place (Jolly).

In other *Gṛhyasūtras* the course of events is described with variations in detail, without altering the overall picture of the ceremony. Some of these features must be mentioned here. At the reception there sometimes occurs a water-consecration (sprinkling with water) (Hillebrandt 52), and a transformation of the fire.

After the initiation the boy is called the "twice-born." While the teacher lays his hand upon the boy, he is regarded as pregnant, and on the third day the Brahman is born. The boys also receive a new name (Oldenberg 466).

After the instruction in duties the teacher kisses the pupil. To the prohibitions already mentioned are added certain food taboos: pungent and salted foods, honey and meat are to be avoided; further, the injunction not to sit on elevated seats and not to go to women. Concerning the conduct of the pupils it is said: they fast silently in the forest, they leave the village, they may not look upon things that hinder study (Hillebrandt 57).

At the concluding ceremony bathing takes place, offerings are made to the dead, *darbha*-grass is planted, the water is set in motion, and a race is held.

At the dismissal of the *brahmacārin*, staff, girdle, and skin — that is, the pupil's attire — are thrown into the water (Hillebrandt 61). The present-day girding customs, which essentially agree with those described in Sanskrit literature and are to be regarded as their direct continuation, show even more clearly than the ancient forms that the ceremony signifies more than admission to instruction — namely, the formal entry of the boy into the community of the father. Particularly significant is the boy's final meal from the mother's plate, which endures for the duration of the festival, in contrast to the brief period of study that is thereby inaugurated (Jolly 583). In the sixteenth or eighteenth year the ceremonially connected first shaving of the beard takes place (Hillebrandt 50).

Girls also undergo an initiation. It is the fertilisation ceremony (*garbhadhāna*) of the bride, which usually takes place immediately after the onset of puberty and marks the beginning of married life (Jolly 583).

The Indian royal consecration, the *rājasūya,* has been discussed by Goldmann in comparison with the Carinthian ducal installation in a comprehensive study, and this later custom has been shown in its fundamental features to be very ancient. I do not enter more closely into this consecration here, since the youth initiation does not stand in direct connection with it.

The reports concerning the classical youth initiations are far less detailed than those concerning the ancient Indian.

The Athenian ephebia became a purely state institution, a military-political preparatory school for future citizens. At eighteen the young man was entered into the citizen roll of his *demos* and received the military cloak, the *chlamys*. As a sign of ephebic status he was publicly presented in the theatre before the assembled people with a spear and shield (Rostovtzev 67). There followed two years of regulated military service, supervised by officials appointed by the state, ten or twelve instructors and a chief leader directing the exercises. Later this institution was brought into immediate connection with higher education and thus became a kind of university corporation, into which even foreigners were admitted, though it remained under state supervision.

The ancient foundation reveals itself in its relation to religious worship. In processions and sacrifices the ephebes participate both in their own name and officially on behalf of the state. Among their special duties are: fetching and escorting the image of Dionysos and the Eleusinian sacred objects; celebrating memorial festivals in honour of the forefathers; conducting the festivals, torch races, ship dances, and elsewhere weapon dances.

After the ephebic period the young men join associations and regularly practice gymnastic exercises. Older men likewise form associations for physical training, often under state supervision; here too connections with religious worship are to be assumed (Usener). The age classes are especially clearly preserved among the Spartans (Nilsson 308), together with very ancient initiation rites. The ephebes are flogged to blood and must remain for a time in solitude. During this period they are required to kill helots.

Similar customs are also transmitted among the Romans. In the temple of Jupiter on the Capitol there was an altar and a chapel of Juventas, later incorporated into the temple and then situated in the vestibule of the cella of Minerva. Here each young Roman who assumed the *toga virilis* paid a tax. The procession that the young men made to the Capitol on this occasion had the purpose of consecrating them to the goddess Juventas (Augustine, *civ.* IV, 11). There is also mention of a cutting of the beard upon entry into manhood.

In the time of Augustus there existed permanent associations of noble youth (*Juventus*) throughout Italy and the western provinces. A closer connection with the Roman military organisation is not to be assumed, but they were incorporated into the urban civic structure by official decree. At their head stood a *magister*, or sometimes two; their office lasted one year. Upon admission the youths were presented with shield and spear (Rostovtzev 67). Their principal occupation consisted in military exercises. Hunting was also eagerly pursued, especially of wild animals (bears). They appeared in public through their games, the *ludi iuvenales*, competitive contests of sacred character (Rostovtzev 89). At major festivals they appeared in their attire: tunic, shield, sometimes spear and helmet.

The similarity with later German folk customs is immediately striking and has been set forth in detail by Usener.

1. South Germanic Leagues and Initiation Rites

There are a few clear testimonies concerning initiations of youths, age-classes, and associations among the ancient Germans, although on the whole they are rather scanty. Above all, some information is found in Tacitus' *Germania*. The entrance into youth was for the free-born boy an important turning point in life. Whereas children grew up together without regard to rank, youth distinguishes the free man from the bondsman (ch. 20).

The free youth becomes a citizen of the state through the solemn presentation of arms. Usually he then departs, while the bondsman generally remains in the household. This significant transformation in the young man's life is expressed by Tacitus in chapter 13 with the words: *"Hitherto they belonged to the household, now to the state."* This opposition has its parallel in the initiations of primitive peoples.

According to chapter 38 of the *Germania*, the free Suebi wore a distinctive hairstyle: the hair was combed sideways and tied in a knot. Among other peoples this special hairstyle is rare and restricted to the period of full manly strength; among the Suebi it was retained even in old age.

The young men thus stand out quite clearly from these brief indications: above all through their capacity for bearing arms, through a special hairstyle, perhaps also through their clothing — the children for the most part went naked (ch. 20) — and they were distinguished from boys and in part also from old men.

The conferring of military status is a solemn act which elevates the young man to citizenship. But by this he has not, as has often been assumed, at the same time passed out of paternal authority. The paternal power — or that of the leader to whom he is handed over by the act of military investiture — is not lifted until the youth leaves the paternal household or that of the leader and establishes his own home.

This is very important: military investiture does not yet mean admission into the class of fully entitled, marriageable men. Thus, the age-class of bachelors, bounded by investiture and marriage, is clearly defined.

Among peoples frequently engaged in warfare, the young men form an association of permanently battle-ready warriors (Schurtz 321). The Germans at the beginning of our era were such a people. The *Gefolgschaft* (war-band) is in essence a fellowship of combatants. It consists mainly of unmarried men, and these also formed the core troops in the army. The entire host was composed of bachelors and married men. In the *Germania* (ch. 7) it is said: to mother and wife the man returns with his wounds.

Of the greatest importance for Germanic initiation is the report on the Chatti warriors (Tacitus, *Germania* ch. 31):

"A custom which is also found among other Germanic peoples, though rarely and as a mark of individual daring, has among the Chatti become habitual: as soon as they have grown to manhood, they let hair and beard grow, and only after they have slain an enemy do they lay aside this consecrated adornment of the head, by which they pledge themselves to bravery. Over blood and spoil they bare their foreheads; they declare that only then have they earned their life and proved themselves worthy of fatherland and parents. The cowardly and unwarlike keep their hair-mass.

"The bravest also wear an iron ring — this is regarded by the people as disgraceful — as a kind of bond, until they free themselves by slaying an enemy. Many of the Chatti take pleasure in this adornment, and now they are grey in this distinction; friend and foe alike point them out. They open all battles; they are always in the front rank, startling in appearance not only in war but also in peace, for even then their facial expression does not soften into a more friendly aspect. None has house or field or any domestic concern. Wherever they go, they are entertained; they squander what belongs to others and are careless of their own affairs, until feeble old age renders them unfit for the hard life of war."

The significance of this report for Germanic youth initiation has not yet been fully appreciated. In the following, some important indications in this direction will be adduced, such as those given by D. A. Kauffmann, Fustel de Coulanges, Hammarstedt, Hermann Fischer; yet conclusions have not been drawn from these indications. Above all it is important that none of the reported facts stands isolated within Germanic tradition.

Other accounts likewise speak of the fearsome appearance of attacking Germanic warriors, who intentionally made themselves as terrifying as possible. And precisely the shaggy Chatti warriors open the battle.

The leaders of the Suebi (Tacitus, *Germania* 38) arranged their topknot with particular care: *"This is a matter of adornment, yet not without significance. For not in order to love or to be loved, but in order to appear the taller and more formidable and to inspire terror, they comb and bind their hair when they go into battle, and they do so carefully for the eyes of the enemy."*

To illustrate this effect, one may compare the description given by Ammianus Marcellinus (around 400 A.D.) of the Alemannic prince Chnodomar: "*Chnodomar, who wore a red-gleaming tuft of hair upon his crown, marched at the head.*" The Harii appeared with their black shields and painted bodies — likewise the Britons, Caesar (*Bell. Gall.* 5, 14), painted themselves dark blue in order to appear more terrible — so that to the enemy they seemed almost a *feralis exercitus*.

The requirement for young warriors to have slain an enemy is by no means isolated; the same is reported of the Scythians and of several peoples of lower culture.

Somewhat more difficult is the assessment of those warriors who persist in their wild appearance and devote themselves to warfare for life, remaining unmarried and without property or land. The cowardly and the unwarriorlike also do not cut their beard and hair. At first this means that such men were not admitted into the general male class of the Chatti, into which one was incorporated by shaving and cutting the hair. Müllenhoff (D. A. IV, 416) believes that the brave distinguished themselves sufficiently from the cowardly within the company of the shaggy-haired by the wearing of the ring.

But only of the bravest is it said that they consecrated themselves by wearing a ring — and, as one must assume, to the god of war or of the dead; among the Chatti this was Wodan (Tacitus, *Germania* 9, 2). This act of consecration becomes clearer if one considers more closely the letting-grow of the hair.

Parallels to hair- and beard-cutting or to the letting-grow of the hair have already been assembled by Müllenhoff. After a victory over the Roman legions the Batavian leader Civilis — the Batavi being a branch of the Chatti — cut his hair in accordance with a vow he had made, having let it grow until then.

The best-known example is King Harald Fairhair, who remained uncombed until, according to his oath, he had won sole rule over Norway. Among the Romans, the letting-grow wild of the hair was a sign of mourning. Müllenhoff (D. A. IV, 415) also points to the haircut at entry into the ephebate among the Greeks, and at adoption and assumption of arms among the Lombards and Franks.

"Among the Chatti there was thus a general custom intensified in a warlike manner, and the performance of the haircut was linked to the fulfilment of a vow. If the Chatti let their hair grow from the time of entry into the ephebate, then the final haircut was performed at that point, certainly with a special religious solemnity to which a vow was attached."

2 **Remaining in a state of wildness and a period of instruction and probation in war**, which appears to conclude through proof of martial capability, through the killing of an enemy and the acquisition of booty.

3 **Cutting of hair and beard**, whereby incorporation into the fully entitled men is sealed.

Yet the account of Chapter 31 is not exhausted by this. In Chapter 13 of the *Germania* we learn of the beginnings of a warrior retinue. In contrast to this stand decisively the Chatti warriors, whom one has often called "professional warriors." This warrior class creates no conditions from which a hereditary warrior estate might develop. They form a military celibacy and may be compared with the Nordic berserkers (Hammarstedt 118), though this comparison has been rejected from many sides. Müllenhoff (D. A. IV, 418) rejects the comparison with the berserkers on the grounds that they share only celibacy with the Chatti warriors. Krüger's comparison of the Chatti warriors with an order of mendicant monks likewise goes too far.

Delbrück (p. 46) finds Tacitus' description "*questionable insofar as it elevates the Chatti too far above the other Germans. Nowhere do historical facts show that one Germanic people was essentially more capable than another.*" It is not a matter of a specific peculiarity of warfare.

"That upon the ground of general Germanic warfare vagabonds, adventurers, robbers and parasites moved through the districts without family, fixed residence, or steady work, returning only occasionally to their kin, yet when it came to fighting being the first in attack and gladly placing themselves in the foremost line of the wedge formation — that such fellows, who sometimes also took Roman pay, occurred in numbers among all Germanic peoples, one may readily believe. But by calling these wildlings 'professional warriors,' one must not turn the other Germans into peasants; it is only a difference of degree — they are all warriors."

This view is untenable already on the basis of the *Germania* text. One can show that the institution of the Chatti warriors does not stand as isolated as it first appears.

Far more penetrating is what Fustel de Coulanges (771) says about the Chatti warriors. They are a distinct class of warriors. They are consecrated to war; Coulanges bases himself on the words *votivum obligatumque virtuti*. *Votivus* has the following sense: *"It is said of one who has been dedicated beforehand to a god, one who truly belongs to the god."* What Tacitus here calls *virtus* is not abstract bravery, but bravery conceived personally and divinely — it is the divinity of valour. These men are bound by a vow to the god of war. For them combat is thus a religious obligation (773). The vow does not always occur with the consent of the consecrated; for according to Tacitus the cowards have the same appearance and must remain by compulsion in the warrior body.

Perhaps these men were dedicated to war from birth. These warriors, who stand in the forefront in battle, are not maintained by the state but live from the hospitality of the peasants, which according to Tacitus' report must often have been burdensome; and it was custom to receive and feed them. Coulanges poses the question (775) whether it was law, religion, or some power that obliged the peasants to do so.

It seems to me that originally religious reasons were decisive. It gives the impression that these lifelong warriors constituted a *männerbund* which, as known among non-civilised peoples, carried out the youth initiation. Not only military celibacy — which reappears, for example, among the Jomsvikings and much later in the trading companies of the Hanse — makes this probable, but also their distinctive appearance, which, as shown above, places them in particularly close relation to the other world, to which we shall return especially in connection with the Harii, and above all their being entertained.

That they were permitted certain liberties may be inferred from the word *prodigus*; they demanded abundant, even lavish, provisioning. This cannot be explained by saying they were feared for their bravery — the peasants were themselves warlike enough to drive away unwelcome guests — but is understandable only from religious obligation. This too will be further substantiated.

The treatment of the cowards is not yet entirely clarified, though Coulanges has pointed out a path. I do not believe they were such as were consecrated against their will or from birth. Originally all youths pledged their lives, and the capable redeemed this pledge through the life of an enemy.

But whoever could not redeem it — that is, the cowardly and unmartial — was not admitted into the class of men. They remained burdened with an unfulfilled vow-debt, left to the warrior league, and it is not improbable that they were sacrificed. (The few uninitiated "wild ones" are without rights and are soon disposed of.)

I therefore interpret Tacitus' report on the Chatti warriors as meaning that this people possessed a warlike men's league of religious foundation, which carried out the youth and men's initiation and thereby undertook the formation of youths into fully capable citizens. The religious significance of the Chatti league did not lie entirely open to view, but could easily be inferred. It will become even clearer through comparison with another Germanic warrior troop.

In chapter 43 of the *Germania,* Tacitus reports the following about the Harii:

"Moreover, apart from their strength, by which they surpass the peoples just previously enumerated, the Harii are fierce and seek to enhance their innate wildness by art and by well-chosen time: their

shields are black, their bodies painted; they choose dark nights for battle and by the dreadful and shadowy appearance of their ghostly army they inspire terror."

Müllenhoff (D.A. IV, 492) explains *feralis exercitus* as a "host of spectres," a procession of *lemures* and *larvae*, "spirits of the dead." The comparison with a host of the dead would thus go back to Tacitus himself. At the same time, reference is made to a passage in Lombard law according to which a perpetrator disguises himself, renders his face unrecognisable, and thus sets out for plunder. I shall return to this later. Schwynzer adds to the above explanation:

"Perhaps, however, it is not a Roman but a Germanic conception that underlies this: the black host could well have appeared to the enemy as an actual army of the dead."

Is it likely that Tacitus himself arrived independently at this comparison? He did not know the black host of the Harii from personal observation; his informants must have told him of the terror of the "army of the dead" (Künnerkopf 20, N. J.).

To resolve this question, one must first consider the transmitted facts: the Harii surpass the other peoples in strength and attack at night in masks. If the expression *feralis exercitus* accords with these facts also from inner considerations, then it will not merely be a poetic comparison; rather, an underlying reality must have existed.

Masking in itself already points to a religious connection; by it "someone" was to be represented. For from what has been said above one must assume with Wundt that the use of the mask merely to render oneself unrecognisable is secondary.

In the appearance of the Harii, as Weniger remarks (p. 209), we are not dealing with a one-time stratagem of war, but with an established custom. Accordingly, it must rest upon an agreement once fixed for future cases. In such an undertaking there must have prevailed a certain conviction — to be what one represented, namely a host of spirits. Thus some kind of obligation or vow must have lain at its basis, among themselves as well as toward the powers of the spirit world, whose role they enacted and which could hardly be imitated by others except their own people. This last remark seems to me quite conclusive; it clearly characterises the attitude of simple peoples toward the world of demons. This has persisted in our own folk custom down to the most recent times (cf. p. 50). Weniger then briefly refers to the Chatti warriors, without drawing further conclusions. The report of their particular strength also seems well founded. The name *Harii* means "belonging to the army or to war." Probably the Harii were not a separate tribe, but merely the warriors of the Lugii. What Tacitus recounts about their manner of fighting suggests that by their very name they were intended to be designated as the army itself, as the core troop, as the ghostly host. Likewise, the members of the Nordic host of the dead are called *einherjar*, "chosen avengers" (cf. HR Chatti).

Weniger further compares (loc. cit.) the *feralis exercitus* with the white army of the Phocians in their battle against the Thessalians (Herodotus VIII, 27). In that case it was a stratagem of war. On the advice of a clever man the Phocians smeared their bodies white with gypsum and attacked their terrified enemies by moonlight. According to Weniger, the effectiveness of this ruse was greatly aided by the local tradition (Parnassus). In essence it was an imitation of the orgies of Dionysus on Parnassus (p. 231). According to the tradition, Dionysus Zagreus grew up there and was torn apart by the Titans, who had whitened themselves with gypsum. Zagreus was then restored to life by Zeus.

Building upon this belief one could resort to this stratagem of war; the psychological foundation is therefore, according to Weniger, the same as in the *exercitus feralis*.

One is tempted to seek the similarity of the two armies still more deeply and to suppose that that white army was not merely the invention of a clever man, but rather the core troop of the Phocians attacking in their ritual attire.

Miss Harrison (*Themis* 16 ff.) has interpreted the story of Zagreus as a form of initiation rite. The killing and reviving, the colouring of the killers with gypsum — the newly initiated mystics also paint themselves white — are the principal points of comparison with the initiation of uncivilised peoples. It is striking that a child is killed; but this may be explained as follows: the Greeks had abandoned the initiation of youths, but had transferred the rites into childhood (20).

Here too we are dealing with warriors who attack in disguise, which they otherwise use in cult dances. It may be inferred that the content of their performance was an initiation rite. This does not stand alone in Greek tradition. The Kouretes — armed youths who are also regarded as demigods, satyrs, sileni, Bacchants and who perform orgiastic dances — have the initiation to carry out as *paidophoroi* (*Themis* 25). They originated as men and were only later received into the circle of the gods. Later, the invention of the weapon-dance is ascribed to them. They are also regarded as nature spirits and promoters of animal fertility. "Kouretes" is the name of a civic association devoted to cultic purposes which celebrates the festival of Artemis in Ephesos. They have often been confused and intermingled with the Korybantes and other daemons (Pauly–Wissowa). The Korybantes were represented by the Korybantiones. Of them an initiation custom is transmitted: the new *mystes* sat upon a throne and was danced around.

These parallels also make it probable that the Harii formed a religious association. What must be inferred about them is reported of the Chatti.

Probably the consecration of the Chatti to the god of death and war, Wodan, essentially means nothing other than that during the period of their vow they represented ancestral and death-spirits. Their appearance suggests this. A brief survey of the letting of the hair grow in Germanic tradition showed that wildness is a condition in which one can enter into connection with the other world — according to the two tales with Hell and the Devil. A conception that is entirely common among primitive peoples. Among the peoples of antiquity, through neglect and dirt one comes into connection with the souls of the departed.

This notion has its ultimate basis in the fact — as was set forth in the first chapter — that remaining in the most neglected condition produces ecstatic excitations. A kind of ecstasy also played a certain role among the warriors under discussion; this will become clearer later. Thus their great strength and ability to form the core troop of the army would also be explained.

If the religious foundation of the fighting style of the Harii is now established, nothing is said in the tradition about their relation to the initiation of youths. Since they formed the core troops and possessed this religious significance, one may conclude that they also solemnly initiated the young men.

The suggested Greek parallels show that Germanic associations and their relation to youth initiation are not isolated even within the Indo-European peoples. Much more important for the evaluation of Germanic conditions, however, are two reports about Germanic tribes from the fourth and sixth centuries after Christ. Ammianus Marcellinus (31, 9, 5) reports of young warriors of the Taifali who, though made capable of bearing arms, remain dependent upon older warriors until they free themselves through a brave deed accomplished alone — by killing a boar or a bear. In Procopius (*de bello Persico* II, 25), the young warriors of the Heruli, whom he calls slaves, must enter battle without defensive weapons and only when they have proven themselves capable warriors does their lord permit them to carry a shield in battle. Both passages — whose significance for the Germanic probationary period between military majority and full adulthood was emphasised by R. Pallmann — also report initiation rites:

1 the killing of powerful animals, whereby the slaying of the bear recalls the tale of the Bearskin;

2 fighting without defensive weapons, thus under extraordinary conditions.

The report about the Heruli, who came from southern Scandinavia, is at the same time evidence for this institution in the North; they will not have learned this custom only in the South. The Taifali were most probably a branch of the Lugian-Vandals and thus also originated in the North. The cynocephali of the Lombards will be discussed later (p. 49).

Tacitus therefore reports, for the first century after Christ, of warrior-bands with religious foundations, which at the same time formed the core of the army and had the education of the male youth in their hands. From the Chatti we further learn details of the life of the association: the Chatti warriors are propertyless bachelors who live from the generosity of their fellow tribesmen. Similar institutions are known from the fourth to the eighth centuries.

2. The Nordic Tradition

The Chatti warriors have often been compared — despite numerous objections, yet, as I believe, with good reason — to the Nordic berserkers. But the comparison was never based on a precise investigation and systematic juxtaposition.

Concerning the berserkers, a great number of reports have been preserved in the Old Norse sagas, both in the historical sagas — the *Íslendingasögur* and *Konungasögur* — as well as in the largely mythical so-called *Fornaldarsögur*, which treat the time before the settlement of Iceland. The period in which these sagas were written down extends over three centuries (approximately 1200-1500). Particularly in the *Fornaldarsögur*, many younger motifs were incorporated.

Firm chronological points within the tradition are offered by the accounts of Saxo Grammaticus (around 1200) and Snorri Sturluson (1230) concerning the berserkers. The latter essentially agree with the Icelandic sagas. Saxo does not know all the features of the Icelandic conception; his understanding corresponds most closely to the medieval Danish view, *"in which the berserker rage is not known as a disease with a specific name, definite symptoms, and connected to the nature of particular individuals, but rather as a frenzy which can break out in various persons when external or internal motives call it forth"* (Olrik, *Kilderne til Sakses* I, 57 ff.). This is very important. The Danish conception appears, on the one hand, to be a weakening of the older idea; on the other hand, it shows that the berserkers were not, as for example Mogk believes, purely mythical figures.

In what follows I shall repeatedly have to return to the investigations of Axel Olrik, *Kilderne til Sakses oldhistorie* I, II, and *Danmarks Heltedigtning* I, II. Through these works one gains a clear picture of the intellectual climate of the age of our sources. All heroic poetry — popular as well as foreign elements — is reshaped into new ideals.

The Old Norse berserkers are mighty warriors. *Berserkr* means "a warrior clothed in a bearskin." They also wore coats of wolf fur instead of mail shirts and were therefore also called *úlfhéðnar*. Moreover, they possessed the ability to fall into a state of ecstasy, in which they became superhumanly strong and invulnerable. They are usually portrayed as unmarried, dangerous swashbucklers.

They most often appear in groups — in twos, in fives; very frequently they are twelve. They generally stand in the service of a king (rarely of a farmer, cf. above) and form his core troops.

They are the first in battle; thus, for example, of King Harald Fairhair's berserkers it is said: *"No iron bit them, and wherever they stormed forward, no one held his ground."*

Yet they also appear as robbers and criminals acting on their own. Their bad reputation stems chiefly from this, but also from their general violence. Thus, for example, in *Örvar-Odds Saga* 24 it is said: *"I heard that these (berserkers) are of all men the most malicious and the least inclined to accomplish anything good."*

According to the narrative of *Hrólfs Saga Kraka,* the twelve berserkers of King Aðils devastated his land after he had driven them from his court (chs. 12–15). Almost formulaic and fairy-tale-like are the stories of maidens who are threatened by berserkers — just as otherwise by giants and monsters — and are freed by some hero (cf. *Víga-Glúms Saga* 4; *Hrólfs Saga Kraka* G., p. 34; *Egils Saga* 64; *Flóamanna Saga* 15).

Finally, however, there are also berserkers who practice *berserkergang* only in their youth and later become good citizens. The best-known example of this is Úlfr, the father of Skallagrímr. It is said of him that he was a berserker. But after he had ceased to go on Viking expeditions, he became a very capable farmer.

His peculiar nature is described in detail: *"but whenever evening came on, he became so ill-tempered that few people could speak with him. As it grew dark he tended to grow drowsy. People say that at night he often went about in altered shape."* People called him

Kveld-Úlfr, that is, "Evening Wolf" (*Egils Saga* I). Only once more, shortly before his death, did he fall into berserker rage (*Egils saga* 27).

In the *Eyrbyggja Saga,* chapters 25–28 tell of two berserkers who would gladly be rid of their masters — four are mentioned in total. With their last master, a large landowner in Iceland, one of them wishes to marry his daughter, and since he possesses no wealth, he intends to earn his bride through labour. Children of berserkers are also often mentioned, for example the daughter and the son of the berserker Hromund (*Hálfs Saga,* ch. X).

In the end, people believe in the inheritance of berserker nature, yet it is frequently portrayed as diminishing, so that the descendants are regarded merely as "very brave." The decline of berserker strength is clear in the descendants of Kveldulf. His son Skallagrim and his grandson Egil still have extraordinarily strong fits of rage — Skallagrim raged in a manner similar to a berserker (*Egils Saga* 27; 40) — but they are no longer considered berserkers in the same sense as Ulf himself.

Finally, in later usage the word *berserkr* simply means "strong fighter."

The actual attack of berserker fury is called in Old Norse *berserksgangr,* and it is described with remarkable consistency. For example, in *Ynglinga Saga* 6: *"His men fought without armour and were mad like dogs or wolves; they bit their shields and were strong like bears or bulls. They killed men, but neither fire nor iron could harm them. This is called berserkergang."*

In agreement with this description, *Vatnsdæla Saga* 45; *Kristni saga* 2; *Þáttr Þorvalds ens víðförla* 3 relate that they walked barefoot through fire and could be killed only with clubs. They could even throw themselves upon their own swords without being harmed. Only Saxo Grammaticus reports in two passages (326, 328), in describing a berserker attack, that they also swallowed glowing coals. In such a fit they raged even against themselves, against trees and stones.

Tradition clearly shows that this frenzy was connected with animal possession. At least in part, their habit of eating raw meat and drinking blood (see *Hrólfs Saga Kraka* p. 16; *Örvar-Odds Saga* 18) is related to this. I shall return to that later. This animal possession ultimately rests upon disposition and often overcomes the berserker unexpectedly and against his will (*Vatnsdæla Saga* 37). Yet it can also be deliberately induced through the putting on of animal skins — at the very least prepared and initiated by it. Earlier I spoke of the suggestive power of masks. Putting on the bearskin glove immediately brought about animal possession in the shaman (p. 22). I would compare this with how Queen Hvít transformed her stepson Björn into a bear (*Hrólfs Saga Kraka* 19). She strikes him with a wolf-skin glove and utters a curse. Although this account is altogether fairy-tale-like, it nevertheless seems, as becomes clear from what has been said, to rest upon an experience.

The following consideration also supports the assumption that wolf- and bear-skins were essential to the attack. Otherwise it is emphasised of particularly brave warriors that they bared their naked chest to the enemy (cf. Tacitus, *Germania* 6; *Histories* 2, 22). The superhumanly strong berserkers apparently could not do this.

Finally, the Old Norse word *hamask* — "to assume the outward form of another, to fall into *berserkergang*" — and *hamr* — "outer covering, protective spirit" — indicate that the covering with a special outer form produced a condition interpreted as transformation. Compounds with *hamr* point in the same direction: *hamrammr,* "one who can transform into an animal"; *hamnskipti,* "to be now animal, now human, to change shape"; *hamhleypa,* "a person who runs about in another form (shape)." A standing designation of the berserker is also *eigi einhamr,* "not having only one form."

The following accounts are clear: in *Völsunga Saga* VIII, wolfskins (*úlfshamr*) hang over sleeping men. Sigmund and Sinfjötli put them on and become wolves. In *Hrólfs Saga Kraka* 20 it is said of Björn: *"steypti síðan bjarnarhamrinn yfir hann, ok gengr björninn svá út"* — *"He then pulled the bear-skin over himself and went out as a bear."* (Naturally, the many other *hamir* of the sagas are to be compared.) I will not enter into non-Germanic parallel ideas here — the belief in werewolves is extraordinarily widespread — I mention only the Latin *versipellis,* "werewolf," literally "one who changes his skin." The importance of the garment in transformation is still fully recognised when it is burned in order to escape the magical compulsion to transform (e.g., *Völsunga Saga* 8; Grimm, p. 151). Perhaps the belief that the eye does not change during transformation is also connected with this.

With time, however, the importance of the entire garment for transformation fades from consciousness: once it is no longer something experienced but merely retold as a "motif." Thus the garment shrinks to a belt of wolfskin, to the wolf-skin glove, and finally — though rarely — disappears altogether. Often older and newer conceptions stand side-by-side, as in *Hrólfs Saga Kraka*.

It is entirely probable that the capacity for ecstasy in berserkers was deliberately intensified — I shall speak of this again. An ecstatic disposition in general played a great role among warriors; one may compare the Javanese "running amok" (cf. Fischer, Güntert).

In later times, *berserkergang* was legally forbidden (*Grágás* I, 23) and threatened with outlawry within a certain district. The same penalty threatened the men present unless they could bind the berserker. But if it occurred repeatedly, the punishment applied even if they succeeded in restraining him.

This law, together with the medieval Danish conception of

berserkerism described by Olrik, the statement that berserkers were especially weak and powerless after an attack (e.g., *Egils saga* 27; *Eyrbyggja Saga* 28), and the frequent description of their pale appearance, prove them to be human beings.

But since the capacity for ecstasy belongs to the very nature of these warriors and ecstasy possesses strong religious significance, it is not surprising that tradition in part also regards the berserkers as purely mythical beings.

In the *Ynglingasaga* 6 the berserkers are described as Odin's warriors. At first, one should not place too much weight on this isolated statement. Its credibility must first be examined. In this account Snorri portrays the gods as human chieftains who, by virtue of their magical arts, were worshipped like gods. Odin is here probably attributed with berserkers because earthly kings had such excellent warriors around them. But even in the ancient god-poems Odin gathers warriors about himself. These warriors, the *einherjar* ("chosen champions"), are described by Snorri elsewhere (*Gylfaginning* 38-41) in agreement with the Eddic poems. The comparison between berserkers and *einherjar* suggests itself for two reasons. First, as emphasised, because of their ecstatic endowment they could be regarded as supernatural beings. (Their bad reputation is only a later development.) Furthermore, they were the chosen warriors of kings. It is quite conceivable that, in general, the core troops of earthly warriors served as models for the host of the dead (*einherjar*).

The relations of the berserkers to the host of the dead and to the other world can, however, be defined more precisely. Especially in what follows, the purely mythic idea lies very close to lived experience, and one clearly feels how immediate experience is gradually rationalised and mythologized.

Alongside the belief in the capacity for transformation there exists another notion: namely, that the soul — conceived in bodily terms — separates itself from the body and performs great deeds, while the body remains at home as if lifeless, or at least in a sleep-like, dreamlike state. A clear example of this appears again in *Hrólfs Saga Kraka* (23). The berserker Böðvarr Bjarki, the best of heroes, sits quietly in the hall, but outside with the king an enormous bear fights, striking down the enemies in marvellous fashion. When Böðvarr, against his will and at Hjálti's urging, goes out into the battle, the bear disappears — and with it the success of the fight.

This tale is a typical example of persons who are not *einhamr* (not confined to a single bodily form).

In essence it is the same when it is said of Odin: "*When Odin changed his form, his body lay as if sleeping or dead; but he himself was a bird or a wild animal, a fish or a serpent.*" (*Ynglingasaga* 7)

The story of Böðvarr Bjarki clearly shows the close kinship of the berserker with the werewolf conception: either the soul roams about as a wolf while the body remains at home, or men themselves transform into wolves by putting on a belt of wolfskin. (Mogk, *Grundriß* III, §32, even describes berserkism outright as a werewolf myth.) Accordingly, werewolves are regarded in folk belief as soul-, pressure-, and nightmare-spirits.

In the *Hervarar saga* it is said of Angantýr and his eleven brothers: "*It was their custom, when they were alone and felt that the berserkergang would come upon them, to go ashore and fight against trees and great stones. For it had happened that they slew their own men and destroyed their own ships*" (*Hervarar Saga* 2). This raging against trees and stones recalls not only the frenzy of the German Wild Hunt, but is also a habit of the alpine spirits just mentioned.

Very striking is also the similarity between the conduct of the twelve sons of Arngrim and the Indian Maruts, twelve demonic youths, companions of Indra, who as storm deities — often compared with the Wild Hunt — break trees and hurl rocks. But beyond these obvious similarities there are also more concealed threads of connection between the sons of Arngrim and the Wild Hunt. Among them are also mentioned the two Haddingjar (Much, *Vandalische Götter*, 25 ff.). Corresponding to them are the Hasdingi, the leading clan of the Lugii.

The Hasdingi live on in German heroic legend as the Harlunge. This name, however, goes back to that of a Lugian tribe, to which the Harii belonged. *Harilungos* could express the same as the tribal name Harjōs, "members of the host"; it may equally mean "of the lineage of the Harii" (Much, loc. cit. 27). If the Harlunge are designated as Harii, one has certainly thought of the *exercitus feralis*. F. Panzer (*Neujahrsblätter*) has demonstrated the Harlunge as representatives of the Wild Hunt without considering this connection of names.

A closer examination of the mythic conceptions connected with the berserkers thus leads back again to the Harii and to the host of the dead, so that the identification of *berserkir* and *einherjar* in the *Ynglingasaga* acquires considerable significance.

A striking similarity with the berserkers is also shown by the dog-headed warriors of the Lombards. Paulus Diaconus (8th century, I, 11) reports of them that, in order to intimidate the people of the Assipitti, they spread the rumour that they had Cynocephali among them who were so savage that they drank the blood of enemies and, if they could get none, their own. Among the Lombards the ferocity with which they fought — Velleius (II, 106) calls them *gens etiam germana feritate ferocior* — may have suggested the idea of transforming into biting or rabid dogs. Perhaps even their older name Vinnili stands in connection with this circle of ideas, since *winnend, winnig* in the older language and still dialectally (cf. Schmeller, Bavarian Dictionary II, 929) is used especially of raging dogs (Much, *Balder*, 109 f.).

The Germanic warrior groups discussed (Chatti, Harii, berserkers, cynocephali) show essential similarities. In all of them one remarkable fact stands out: core troops in terrifying array are in tradition clearly conceived at one time as human warriors and at another as a host of the dead.

The host of the dead is in early Germanic antiquity initially conceived in thoroughly corporeal terms (cf. Neckel). Even in the Wild Hunt, the German host of the dead in later tradition, corporeally conceived dead — and sometimes even living — persons ride along (cf. Hünnerkopf). The term "army of souls" is therefore incorrect for early Germanic antiquity; "ghost army" or "spirit host" is misleading. Even if later it is said that the living can take part in the procession of the dead, this notion was certainly common in ancient times. It was noted above that the core of primitive religious desires lies in reaching the other world, that is, in intercourse with spirits — who, however, were quite definitely conceived as corporeal.

The means employed to bring about this experience have already been discussed; we find them applied among the Germanic warriors as well: masks and the deliberate arousal of ecstasy — which in part is again induced by masks and, among the Chatti, probably by a state of deliberate wildness — and thereby intensified, so that the extraordinary fighting power of these warriors is produced. Among the Harii there is the additional element of attacking at night.

A preference for night attacks may also be assumed among the berserkers, for their strength appears to have been especially great at night. One thinks here of Kveldulf ("Evening Wolf"). His son Skallagrim lifted a great stone at night, when all were asleep — a stone which later four men were unable to raise (*Egils Saga* 30). And in chapter 40 it is said of him: *"In the evening after sunset, Grim became so strong that he raged against his son."* Moreover, the berserkers are fond of attacking at Yule, the chief festival and the most intense season of hauntings (*Grettis Saga* 19; 40; *Svarfdæla Saga* 7; *Víga-Glúms Saga* 6).

What does all this signify? In order to judge these cases, a parallel phenomenon from later folk belief and custom must be consulted. These are the traditions of the Wild Hunt and of the Salzburg–Tyrolean Perchten-runs and related processions. In a lecture on "Myths and Legends of Advent Time" I attempted to show that the narratives of the Wild Hunt developed, at their core, from two experiential realities and were kept alive over long periods by them.

First, the violent storms (especially of the winter half-year), whose roaring repeatedly creates the impression of a raging, clamorous host, and are therefore again and again imagined as being caused by such a host. Second, the cultic dances performed by a wildly raging, disguised troop of youths — the Perchten, Klöpfer, and the like. Both elements merge in the consciousness and in the storytelling of the believer.

The Perchten and the other noisy processions represent the Wild Hunt, the host of the dead, which — like the Perchten —

promotes the fertility of the coming year.

According to folk belief, the Perchten have the right to imitate the Wild Hunt; for other people, especially individuals who wear no masks, are, as numerous stories recount, severely punished for their presumption if they imitate the cries of the Wild Hunt. But only the village youths are permitted to take part in the Perchten-run. If strangers join in, it not infrequently leads to brawls ending in manslaughter (Andree–Eysn 163 ff.). In Switzerland it is precisely the young men or boys who carry out the noisy processions. This points to very ancient foundations. In a tale (Grimm M 776) it is reported from Delligsen near Alfeld in Hildesheim that *"the farmhands from the whole village once came together to imitate the Wild Hunt. The real Wild Hunt also appeared and raged in the air as the farmhands did below in the village, and the Wild Huntsman threw down an old bear's haunch to them."* This story seems like a last memory of former noisy processions of all the bachelors. At the time of the narration the undertaking was already regarded rather as wanton behaviour and mockery of the Wild Hunt and was accordingly punished by the throwing down of a foul-smelling haunch.

Formerly it was custom — and in large part still is — to entertain the performers of such processions. Until recently it was considered an insult to give the Perchten money. They have from of old been entitled to certain cakes and dishes, probably ancient sacrificial foods. If in present-day folk custom it is still quite clear that the Perchten are entertained in thanks for the blessing they ensure for the prosperity of the fields, one must assume that in earlier times the performers of cultic processions were treated similarly. It is therefore easy to understand that both the Chatti and the berserkers — this will become clearer later — did not need to provide for their own sustenance but were generously supported by others. In the case of the Chatti it must further be added for the period of our report that besides their cultic significance they held the education of the young men in their hands and themselves formed the core troop of the army.

In reviewing the nature of the berserkers, the two conceptions that prevail in the sources — of them as human warriors and as mythical beings — were first discussed. Through comparison with similar Germanic phenomena the riddle is resolved in that they originally represented the host of the dead, and thus their dual nature in the consciousness of the narrators is explained. The Germanic comparative material suggests that the berserkers also formed cultic associations; for only thus is their authorisation to represent the host of the dead possible according to primitive belief. Can this assumption also be confirmed by the tradition?

At first it may seem striking that men in animal disguise should represent the dead. All the more so because among the *einherjar*, the actual Nordic host of the dead, nothing of the kind is mentioned. One must however bear in mind that the depiction of the *einherjar* and of their dwelling place Valhalla in our sources is strongly stylised and offers little in the way of original conceptions (Neckel). I need only point to more recent folk belief. The Perchten, for example, for the most part wear animal masks. But already for the Indo-Germanic period Schröder (124 ff.) distinguished five conceptions of the host of the dead:

1 The Wild Hunt (Germanic, Greek, Dionysos Zagreus, Artemis).
2 A male, warlike armed host, perhaps corresponding to a female warlike host in the Amazons of Artemis.
3 Ecstatically aroused women in connection with serpents.
4 Animal-shaped, mostly phallic fertility demons.
5 Souls of children.

These five groups may also be regarded as two types, corresponding to today's "beautiful" and "ugly" Perchten: one group of beautifully armed and clothed participants, and a second in a terrifying, wild procession. For the Nordic berserkers the animal-shaped demons come first into consideration. Mannhardt (FWK) interpreted them especially as vegetation demons (rye-wolf, -dog, corn-sow, pea-bear, etc.), but repeatedly emphasised the close connection between vegetation and spirits of the dead — chiefly in the sense that the dead who live beneath the earth promote plant growth and thus in part pass over into vegetation spirits.

Schurtz and after him Schröder (appendix) and more recently Haberlandt (615) see in the animal disguises and the various processions and little dramas of later folk custom remnants of initiation rites of youths, and thus animal masks acquire for these scholars another meaning, namely totemistic. Can one assume this also for the berserkers?

The connection between primitive initiation of youths and totemism is not yet fully clarified. Opinions also differ regarding the nature of the religious system called totemism. The following features, however, seem essential: a tribe or clan, even an individual, venerates an animal, a plant, or an object and feels itself related to it. Yet veneration never applies to the individual creature but to the species. One seeks to make oneself as similar as possible to the totem through masks, imitation, or through the solemn killing and eating of the totem animal. As a rule, however, it must not be eaten. Among members of the same totem there are often strict marriage prohibitions (exogamy). They form a kind of kinship group and a firm association. Totemism also occurs without exogamy (Reuterskiöld, 69, 77). Often, for example by Wundt, the view was maintained that the totem animal was originally the soul-animal (manifest form of the soul) of the ancestor (*Elem. d. V.* Ps. 185).

This must by no means be understood as though the conception of soul-animals always pointed to totemism. The belief that the (corporeal) soul becomes visible as an animal is independent of totemism and appears to be much more widely spread than totemism itself. Only in individual cases can totemistic foundations be demonstrated in our tradition.

If one casts a glance at the kinds of animals in whose shape souls were thought in the North to embody themselves, one finds almost all animals again: bee, butterfly, snake, birds, tame and above all wild animals, bear and wolf (Henzen). In the discussion of the *hamir* ("outer forms") as a means of transformation, various kinds of such coverings were indicated.

In view of this fact, an attempt has been made to explain the idea of the berserkers by assuming that human — especially wild — warriors and the belief in animal-shaped soul-spirits merged in the imagination. Just as Mogk, with regard to the Valkyries, holds the view that they represent a union of human female warriors — for that armed women fought in battle is frequently attested (Weinhold, d. Fr. I, 54 f.) — with female-conceived soul- and protective spirits. How closely Valkyries and berserkers stand to one another in popular consciousness is shown, for example, by the fact that the Valkyrie Hervör is the daughter of the famous berserker Angantyr.

Yet such an explanation does not exhaust the transmitted features of the berserker conception.

They almost always appear in groups and are then usually regarded as brothers. This first expresses the fact that the disposition was inherited and that one thought of berserkerism as restricted to certain families. It is also connected with the conception of kinship as the strongest bond of union. The many bonds of friendship and comradeship among the Vikings, which were concluded in the form of blood-brotherhoods (artificial kinship), show this. The members of the warrior-band of the Jomsvikings were also to avenge one another like brothers. Even the *einherjar* Snorri calls (*Gylfaginning* 20) Óskasynir, "adopted sons" of Odin. At the basis of all this lies something very ancient. Among peoples of lower cultural stages, the initiation of youths often lies in the hands of totemistic tribes or clans. Such clans form, through their common totem, a cultic association.

In the North as well, although only remnants survive, still recognisable traces are to be found. Judging from the name *berserkir* or *úlfheðnar*, above all wolf and bear appear to have been preserved as totem animals. Wolf and bear names, alongside other animal names, are certainly not accidental in the family of the berserker Kveldulf, who is known as a historical person.

Grim, the grandson of Björn Halbtroll, was born with a cheek thickly overgrown with hair and bit into iron. (Gr. L., p. 143.) The weakening of berserker strength among the descendants has already been mentioned and will be discussed further.

The mother of Hrólf (Hrólf from hroð-úlfr) Kraki was called Yrsa, "she-bear." The father of the frequently mentioned Böðvarr Bjarki, "little bear," who in the manner described above was transformed into a bear and then bore a bear's form, was called Björn, "bear," and his wife Bera, "she-bear." Of a berserker in the *Hrólfs Saga* it is said that he was the son of a mare.

Still clearer are the names of the clans Ylfingar and Wulfingas, "Wolves." A Germanic tribe on the coast of Pomerania is called Glomman, "howler," from *glammi*, a poetic expression for "wolf" (Much, *Germ. Osten* 145 ff., 161). These "wolves" stand as enemies opposite the "dogs," the Hundingar. The older name of the Lombards is Vinnili, probably "raging dogs"; of them it is also said that they had frenzied warriors with dog-heads among them.

Just as in the Frankish legend Sigmund and Wolfdietrich descend from wolves, so the royal house of the Frankish Merovingians derives from a bull or boar. (*Lepen* 8.)

Thus, one must also assume for the North a kind of totemistic clans — the use of animal names as personal names in general points to this, as Much (loc. cit.) has suggested — which at the same time formed cultic associations comparable to those of peoples of lower cultural stages. I stress that I express myself cautiously here, for traces of totemism are not yet totemism itself. Since greater insight has been gained into this institution and one sees that it is a complex religious and social system, one no longer believes that totemism constituted a necessary stage in the religious development of all peoples. Yet strong similarities are undeniably present; therefore, for the sake of simplicity, the term "totemistic," with the reservation just indicated, will in the following be used to designate these extremely ancient conceptions within the Germanic tradition.

One sees from this that the animal mask is also very old in the Germanic area. Thus there can be no doubt that the basic stock of the animal masks in the Perchten processions is likewise ancient and indigenous. In this way somewhat greater clarity is brought again into the dispute as to whether the Perchten processions derive merely from Roman calendrical customs or whether they are at least in part indigenous. In *Jul* (p. 22) I raised the question how rural processions with unmistakably religious and cultic significance could have developed on German soil out of the large-scale urban Roman festive activities, and I considered it impossible. This view can now be substantially strengthened.

Haberlandt (627) also touches on this question; for the German customs he assumes an indigenous substratum of a totemistic kind and further emphasises the possibility of very ancient common features between Germans and Romans.

Given the close connection between totemism and ancestor cult, it can now no longer be surprising that the berserkers in animal masks represent the host of the dead.

Another feature handed down about the berserkers now gains significance: it is told that they ate raw flesh and drank blood. At first one might indeed regard this with Müllenhoff (D. A. IV, 346) as a war custom, and it is in fact reported of various other peoples as well. One would sooner accept the eating of raw flesh than the drinking of blood. Yet it is striking that it is precisely of the Ylfing Helgi (*Helgakviða Hundingsbana* II) that this custom is told, that in the *Örvar-Odds Saga* (18) it is called a wolfish one, and that Örvar-Odd swears to abandon it (*Örvar-Odds Saga* 18). The entire Viking law which Örvar-Odd vows to observe is admittedly very humane; nevertheless it is not quite understandable why this should be specially mentioned if it were merely a compulsion of war. In the *Hrólfs Saga* (G., p. 16) the berserkers who eat raw flesh and drink blood are called rather trolls than men. The same habit is reported of the Cynocephali of the Lombards and of the Greek Mainads and Thyiads. If one also considers the widespread belief that the drinking of blood and the eating — especially of hearts — imparts extraordinary courage and strength, one will have to attribute to the custom of the berserkers an originally cultic significance.

In this connection it seems noteworthy to me that Björn forbids his wife Bera (*Hrólfs Saga Kraka* 20) to eat of his flesh when on the next day he is slain in bear-form. When she then, under compulsion, takes two bites into her mouth, two of her children born shortly afterward bear outward bodily signs of their half-animal descent.

Yet another phenomenon shows that the berserkers once formed cultic associations, namely the marauding berserkers. At first glance these seem directly to contradict such an assumption.

But the many reports about the berserkers clearly show degeneration and later brutalisation. Great freedoms could doubtless be permitted to them on account of their religious office and their strength. They were also dependent upon the generosity of others, since they usually possessed no land of their own. One is reminded again here of the Chatti warriors. It has already been stated that their customary provisioning is to be understood only on a religious basis. In their procession, which equates them with the represented host of the dead, they naturally had to receive everything they demanded. In Tacitus we find this custom described as long as the league still stood in bloom and prestige, and it had evidently developed into a kind of customary right, as we still find it exercised on a smaller scale today toward the performers of the old processions in the countryside.

Here I must return to Müllenhoff's view of the Harii (Müllenhoff, D. A. II, 117; IV, 492). He sees in their conduct of war a large-scale brigandage, as one knows it in smaller measure in the Lombard crime *walapauz, walopaus,* where the perpetrator disguises himself and makes his face unrecognisable in order to set out on plunder. That the warfare of the Harii does not consist in mere robberies has already been shown above.

Lombard brigandage seems rather to have developed out of a similar cultic practice as that which characterised the warfare of the Harii. This is all the more probable since the Lombards possessed a type of berserker warrior of particular savagery and probably fought in dog masks. *Walapauz* would then be a similar phenomenon of decline as the marauding berserkers.

Such a development need not surprise. The foundation for it lies in the intermediate period in which the mask-wearers — as is known from the initiation rites of primitive peoples — are permitted to rob, plunder, indeed even to kill. On the one hand this explains it as a final "letting oneself go," on the other hand it is possible only because the disguised were regarded as possessed by gods or as demons. Insofar Schurtz is right when he thinks that the freedom of the candidates to commit all sorts of excesses is meant to mark them as spirits (107). But this is again only one side of the matter.

Among the Indians as well, a typical "licence to excess" has been handed down in connection with the *rājasūya*, the royal consecration. Before the solemn enthronement there takes place a symbolic raid and foray directed against the herds of the king's relatives. Here the religious background is clear, since the raid is undertaken by priests (Goldmann 7). The same survives in final remnants in the installation of the duke in Carinthia (Tag 82). It is a phenomenon that belongs quite generally to periods of transition; one may think of the license before the end of the year, the executioner's meal, and the like.

Other, yet clear, survivals which may be conceived precisely as outgrowths of the freedom of religious leagues and consecration candidates, as in the Nordic cases, have been preserved down to our own time.

Particularly instructive are the reports communicated by Rütimeyer (357 ff.). In the Lötschental the unmarried young men, disguised with wooden masks and sheepskins, and making noise with cowbells fastened to their belts, storm through the village shouting "like the devil." Formerly (even as late as 1860) women and children, as well as young men under twenty, would shut themselves into the houses. At times the masked figures who forced their way into the houses were entertained with meat and "Nideln." *"Begging or even outright robbing no longer occurs, as was formerly the case in the highly instructive customs of the 'Tüfel' of the old Wiler Fastnacht, when the so-called 'putting-right' was recognized — in reality a right of plunder exercised by the masked men in bakeries and butcher shops. Also the stealing of full pots of meat on Fat Thursday before Fastnacht Sunday, reported by Manz among the youths of the Sarganserland, belongs here."*

Of the greatest importance is what Rütimeyer learned (263) concerning the origin of the Lötschental masking customs: it is assumed that they derive from the "Schurtendiebe," who allegedly gathered around the 15th century in the "Dietrich," a small forest clearing on the southern side of the Lötschental. According to legend, the Dietrich was the first place settled by the people of Lötschen; remains of walls can still be seen there. "Schurte" means short coat, and the name "Schurtendieb" may derive from the short sheepskins still worn today by the masked men. These Schurtendiebe, equipped with wooden masks, used to break into the villages by night and rob grain and other goods.

According to another informant, in prehistoric times a band of robbers dwelt in the dense forests on the southern side of the Lötschental, called the "*geschulten Diebe*" ("trained thieves"), so named because members had to prove themselves by leaping, with heavy booty, across the Lonza, the wild glacier stream of the valley, at a place still pointed out today. Only after fulfilling this condition were they admitted. These robbers made a sport of attacking the villages of the valley dwellers. They appeared in terrifying fashion, in shaggy skins, sheepskins, hideous masks, with resounding cowbells, and armed with heavy clubs they stormed the trembling inhabitants in the darkness of night. In the 17th century these raids ceased. The masks are now used only on Fat Thursday, Carnival Monday and Tuesday, in order to frighten people (364). Rütimeyer suspects that this legendary robber band preserves a remnant of rites deriving from age-classes and secret associations. Special weight must be given to the facts that only unmarried young men take part, that a test of courage and strength is reported, and that women, children, and young men under twenty shut themselves in.

In other carnival processions too, the young men are granted considerable liberties: stealing food and wood, breaking and soiling household objects. Yet while, for example, in the Schemenlaufen in Imst (Tyrol) the various masks must renounce excessive license, the "Roller" and "Scheller," who wear

Perchten garments, remain untouched (*Jul* 81, note 253).

Thus over a long period the same phenomenon has persisted. It is understandable that in later times masks, once no longer sacred, could be used spontaneously for criminal purposes. But for the first centuries of our era I consider this excluded; if such acts of robbery are encountered then, they must be regarded as a degeneration of a religious institution. The transformation of religious associations into robber bands is also found among peoples of lower culture.

For the cultic processions of the berserkers, whose degenerate form appears in the marauding berserkers, there is still a historical testimony. First of all, the time at which the berserkers attack — the Yule season — is significant. Perhaps one might explain this as follows: (1) in winter they had time, since no wars were waged; (2) they made use of the Yule season, when people allowed themselves to relax and could more easily be surprised at their feasts.

Moreover, the prevailing folk belief that the Yule season was the most dreadful time of spirits would have aided them. But one cannot stop there. I need only refer to what was said above. Through their close connection with Odin — who in the tradition often appears at the Yule festival and thereafter bears the name Jólnir — they stand in relation to the Yule feast.

From the 10th century we possess a description by the

Byzantine emperor Constantine Porphyrogenitus (912–959) of the so-called Gothic games at Christmas (Sjöberg 34). A foreign people, clearly Germanic, performs its Yule ceremonies before the emperor, though these are frequently interrupted by poetic addresses to him, which form the principal part of the Byzantine court ceremonial. Apart from this, the following remains:

Two divisions, one of the bodyguard and one of the fleet, appear before the emperor with their leaders. On each side stand two men clad in pelts (the hair turned outward), wearing variously formed masks. All are armed with shields and sticks, and while striking their shields with the sticks they cry "*tul*" and perform a ring dance. The four masked men — sometimes also all the performers — are called Goths.

Yet at that time there were no Goths in Constantinople; they had disappeared from the mercenary troops since the 6th century. At that time they were the Russians, that is, the Swedes dwelling in Russia — the Varangians. It is therefore credible that in this report we possess the oldest description of Scandinavian Yule customs. In the 10th century one must imagine these warriors clad in pelts as berserkers.

This is also highly important for judging the Nordic Christmas processions. That these processions — especially the figures wrapped in pelts — appear extremely archaic in the Yule festival of the present day has always been emphasised, and it was difficult to believe that as a whole they were borrowed from

Germany.

Yet they could not be traced back to the age of the sagas. But if berserkers once held processions and performed dances during Yule, then the foundation of the present-day processions is entirely native.

Finally, in the tradition the berserkers are portrayed as heathens. In the *Saga of Ketill hængr* (ch. 5) it is told of the berserker Framar that he was a *blótmaðr,* "a worshipper of heathen gods." Above all, he offered sacrifice to Odin. In a stanza (Egil's Saga 64), placed in the mouth of Egil, it is said that the berserker who is to be mocked by this poem sacrifices to the gods. This stanza, with its contemptuous secondary meaning, cannot have been composed by Egil himself, who was a heathen, but probably stems from the 12th century (Eg. 64, note p. 212). Nevertheless it is important: the berserker is designated a heathen. Likewise, the reports that fire consecrated by the sign of the cross burned the berserkers point to them as "heathens" (cf. Güntert 23).

Very significant is the previously mentioned legal provision. The prohibition of the *berserkergang* stands in a series of outlawed heathen cult acts. Thus even at the time of the compilation of the Icelandic written law there was still the awareness that this concerned something heathen and cultic. That berserkers were in fact once banished we learn from Norway: Eirik Jarl (1014) outlawed all robbers and berserkers

(*Grettis Saga* 19).

I shall now summarise provisionally what has been said thus far about the berserkers.

The berserkers wear bear- and wolf-garments and stand in relation to the host of the dead. Animal disguise and animal-possession, together with animal names as personal and clan names, their appearance in groups as brothers or united by artificial kinship, the eating of raw flesh and drinking of blood, their connection with ancestor worship — all this points to totemistic foundations.

Furthermore, an intimate connection with Odin is evident through the wolf-mask, the capacity for transformation, their relation to the host of the dead, and their appearance at Yule. Extensive freedom under the mask was probably permitted. As a formed association they are consistently unmarried. Initiation rites, to which I shall presently turn, are reported.

Thus, all essential characteristics of cultic male associations are present. That these traits are no longer easily recognisable in our literary sources is self-evident. The period of our reports is the pronounced heroic age; according to them, the remnants of the old associations stand exclusively in the service of war and of a ruling stratum (without pressing that concept too strictly), and thereby lose their comprehensive cultic character. Our sources partly transmit the old tradition in misunderstood, formulaic fashion, and for the most part the truly cultic element recedes strongly into the background.

3. Turning Away from Berserkism

It can likely be assumed that the berserkers once had the initiation of young people in their hands.

When one learns that there were people who lived a berserker life only in their youth and later married and became capable householders, it gives the impression that they passed through their "period of trial" as berserkers, just as later it was customary to do so as Vikings. Ordinarily, the Viking expedition lasted three years; then the young man married and became more or less settled.

If, in the life of the saga age — not only in its fairy-tale elements — the concept of a probationary period between boyhood and mature youth appears as something effectively developed, then in the saga accounts of a trial period we may suspect the half-forgotten preliminary stage. It becomes evident that Viking life has many close points of contact with the older berserker life.

Very often no sharp distinction is made between *víkingr* and *berserkr*. Berserkers are directly called Vikings in *Gunnlaugs Saga Ormstungu* 6; *Hrólfs Saga Kraka* (G.) p. 12; *Flóamanna Saga* 15. In the *Saga of Ketill Hæng* 5 a Viking king Framar is mentioned, yet he is clearly characterized as a berserker (pp. 132, 136). In the *Svarfdæla Saga* 7 it is said: "A man is called Moldi; he is a Viking or a berserker." Likewise in *Örvar-Odds Saga* 19 (= *Fas.* II) a Viking Eyþjófr is described as "a wicked berserker."

The gradual turning away from berserkerism and turning toward Viking life is clearly reflected in the tradition — for example in the descendants of Úlfr the Fearless. In both the one line Úlfr-Hallbera-Kveldulf-Skallagrimr-Egil, the principal heroes of the historical sagas, and in the other line Úlfr-Hallbjörn-Ketill-Grímr-Örvar-Oddr, belonging to the romantic Viking tradition, the berserker disposition gradually fades. The two Gríms are still distinctly half-berserkers. Of Skallagrimr it is told that he was dark and ugly (cf. p. 47), that on his departure for Iceland he had twelve companions with him, all very strong, some of supernatural strength (*hamrammir, Egil's Saga* 25). In *Egil's Saga* 27 it is reported that he raged like a berserker; in *Egil's Saga* 40 he had, after sunset, a fit of fury in which he killed a man and then fell upon his son Egil. When his maid called out to him, *"You are raging!"* — the word *hamast* is used here — he released Egil, pursued the maid, and killed her.

Grímr Loðinkinni is no longer wholly invulnerable, yet partly so. In the Hallbjörn line one sees clearly how later tradition moves the berserkers closer to mythical beings. Hallbjörn is called a half-troll, and Grímr's mother was a troll-woman.

In the fifth generation, Egil and Örvar-Oddr already successfully fight against berserkers; these are among their greatest heroic deeds. When Ormr Stórólfsson the Strong performs an extraordinary feat of strength, it is expressly emphasised that he was the strongest man in all Iceland, in old as in new times, that he was *einhammr* — not a berserker (*Þáttr Orms Stórólfssonar, Flateyjarbók* I, 524; cf. p. 75).

Egil's wild nature reveals itself for the first time when, at seven years old, he kills a playmate who had defeated and mocked him. His mother then says that his *víkingsefni,* his "making of a Viking," is becoming apparent. Örvar-Oddr is the typical Viking hero of legendary tradition. In his saga the departure from the old berserkerism is especially clear, above all in the Viking law that he adopts, which, as Olrik expresses it, sets forth only more humane demands: not to eat raw flesh and not to drink blood; not to rob peaceful merchants, farmers, or women; on pain of death, not to rape a woman (*Örvar-Odds Saga* 18). Otherwise, too, Icelandic literature likes to dwell on noble Vikings (Olrik *Kilderne til Sakses* II, 207; e.g. *Flóamanna Saga* 16).

The close inner relationship between Vikinghood and berserkerism becomes even clearer when one considers the initiation rites and laws of the warrior bands. The most important traditions for this are found in *Hálfs Saga, Hrólfs Saga Kraka,* the laws of King Frothi of Denmark (Saxo, Book V), the *Jómsvíkinga Saga,* and the laws of the Irish warrior band, the Fianna. All these traditions stand in some connection with the berserkers. The selection of the *hálf-rekkar* is undertaken by Steinn, the grandson of the berserker Hromund (*Hálfs Saga* 10). The hero Hrólfr Kraki and the band of warriors at King Frothi's court are berserkers, and the Fianna too stand in connection with berserkerism. In the *Jómsvíkinga Saga* there is no longer any explicit mention of this, yet details of its regulations correspond with the laws of the *hálf-rekkar*.

Axel Olrik (*Kilderne til Sakses* II, 196 ff.) has compared and closely examined the Viking laws, proceeding from the laws of Frode. The results and points of view of this work form the foundation for further investigation, and I will briefly summarise the main points here.

Three bodies of legislation are attributed to the Danish King Frode: a Danish, a Norwegian, and a Russian one, which he is said to have issued during his war expeditions. However, these laws are not based on actual historical events in the same way as, for example, the laws of the Jomsvikings. Frode's laws are not to be regarded as a unified legal document, nor could such a document have been preserved unchanged through oral transmission. Rather, his laws must be understood as a collection of legal provisions, of which it is known only that they were ascribed to the legendary King Frode.

The Norwegian law contains only provisions concerning theft and represents an abstract-poetic expression for security during the so-called "Frode peace."

The "Russian" law is the most important for the present study, since it is identical with the law of the Halsrekkar (206). It represents the law of a Viking war band, such as frequently occurred in the Viking Age; the best-known example is that of the Jomsvikings. Beyond the provisions of the Jomsvikings, nothing is known from historical warrior associations; what has otherwise been transmitted is not binding for a specific circle of warriors. In the poetically constructed associations, however, all the more trials of prowess are mentioned.

A significant advance beyond such isolated demands is represented by the Hals-law in its regulations governing conduct toward women (not to violate captives, not to dishonour the wife of another man, to acquire a maiden only through lawful bride-price with the father's consent). This development reaches completion in later poetry in the Viking law of Hjalmar (*Örvar-Odds Saga* 18).

Outside Scandinavia, similar regulations are found in the voluntary warrior association of the Irish Fianna (207). Only the marriage law is altered there: the command to pay bride-price is transformed into a prohibition against accepting a dowry.

Thus, the same law appears under different names among Norwegians, Danes, and Irish. However, the heroes of Hrolf and Frode, as well as those of the Fianna, are known only in the poetic sphere; they are the ideal warrior bands of heroic poetry.

The King Frode who stands at the head of such a band is not the same figure to whom the Frode peace is attributed. Apart from him, the Danish Skjöldung tradition knows only one King Frode, who is called "the Generous" among the Danes and "the Brave" among the Icelanders. Of his heroes only Starkad is known. That he had around him a troop of berserkers or chosen warriors, among whom Starkad was the most outstanding, is told in the Icelandic *Skjöldunga Saga* (*Arngr*. 7). It is likely that the laws of the Halsrekkar were derived from this warrior band of King Frode and Starkad; however, the *Hálfs Saga* preserves these laws in their purest form (209).

Finally, the Danish law is composed of various separate laws. It contains the following groups of provisions:

a) property not to be concealed,
b) marriage regulations,
c) various war laws.

Various war laws, which were probably no longer in full force, merged with the ideal demand corresponding to the Frode peace, and thus the Danish legislation came into being. These war laws are, however, all laws of the *comitatus*. That laws arising from real life entered into this series of legendary laws is explained by the fact that they were mixed together with the provisions of the ideal Viking band. The marriage regulations, finally, stem from the laws of the ideal Viking associations.

In saga tradition, therefore, ideal and practical legal principles operate side-by-side. The ideal Viking band is a product of the world of ideas. Yet in the detailed elaboration of particulars, rules deriving from reality are transmitted — rules that would otherwise have disappeared entirely from memory had they not found refuge within these ideal laws.

The opposite is true of the *comitatus* laws: they originate in practical reality. Over time, however, only some of them continue to be observed and gradually become ideal laws.

In later periods they serve as models, because they expressed a high sense of honour grounded in recognition of manly deed — a perspective that retains validity in every age. Thus it is easy to understand how both ideal Viking laws and *comitatus* laws were attributed to the mythical lawgiver Frode (216).

Olrik's investigation allows us a deep insight into the inner development and transformation of the age reflected in our traditions. One sees how far the bearers of this tradition had removed themselves from the cult and the religious binding force of the old associations. Yet these Vikings of the ancient tradition still stand so close to it that its symbols and rites are also taken up into the idealising poetry.

Olrik has also indicated how earlier laws, once they fall out of force, easily become legendary and in part ideal demands. The path by which one can extract from the web of tradition and ideas those features that preserve the reflection of real conditions is clear: the individual details must be examined and compared, for they derive from real life and from unstylised popular tradition. But the totality of the laws must also once more be considered.

First, something must be said about the Fenians (Fianna). Zimmer has assumed (*ZfdA* vols. 32, 33, 35) that among the Fenians of the younger Irish heroic saga one should understand Nordic Vikings.

The battle-fury of the hero Cúchulainn is a depiction, translated into Celtic imagination, of berserker rage. Thus fury and frenzy are also connected among the Irish with the Fenians.

Among the Irish, Norwegians, and Danes three provisions occur in common:

1 Marriage regulations (cf. above),
2 Not to violate women,
3 Not to flee even before nine, eleven, or three opponents.

If one combines points 1 and 2 generally as marriage regulations, then marriage provisions and the demand for bravery and steadfastness are two prescriptions that by no means need belong only to a purely fictional community; indeed, regulations concerning marriage and military fitness belong among the typical competences of men's warrior associations.

The particular form of the marriage regulations, however, seems to belong to the wishes and ideals of a later age. Above all the demands of the Danish law of Frode — that (1) a woman may marry by her own decision even against her father's will, (2) that a man must marry the girl he has first seduced, and the provision of the Fianna not to accept a dowry — stand in sharp contradiction to the otherwise known Old Norse conception of marriage.

It is very instructive what one further learns in this connection from the Irish association: no maiden might be married without asking whether she had a lover among the Fianna; and if that were the case, a payment had first to be made before she might marry (Zimmer, *Keltische Beiträge* III, 1 ff.).

Exactly the same is reported in Book V of Saxo concerning the conduct of the berserkers: "*They did not allow maidens to marry until they had sacrificed their chastity to them. No one might give his daughter in marriage unless he had first purchased their (the berserkers') favour and grace; no one might take a wife unless he had first dearly bought her consent.*" (Herrmann I, 167.)

This is the same right that even today the young men of village communities in the Alpine lands and in Scandinavia possess over the girls of their community: the right to consort with them and to watch over them — that is, not to allow a stranger access to them unless he had, as it were, bought his way in by money or brandy.

A series of wedding customs — such as payments to the young men's associations (in Switzerland), or the blocking of the bridal procession, where the bridegroom must purchase passage with money — are remnants in which the old privileges still show themselves. Both traditions thus rest upon the right of the "*Kiltgang*" or, in the North, the right of premarital access. Especially the report in Saxo, in which even a series of cruelties are recounted corresponding to initiation customs, shows this clearly. Even into modern times in Sweden the younger men were admitted to such rights only after undergoing various tests of manliness (Erixon, 109).

From this old and peasant custom the new age in literature turns away and establishes new marriage regulations. One may ask whether Christian ideas are not already playing a role here. The prerogative of the young men over the maidens of the community entails fairly strong endogamy, and the Church sought to combat marriages among close relatives. I shall return to Saxo's account later; as will be shown, it is exaggerated not only because of the newer attitude of the age and Saxo's own character, but also because of the dramatic situation of the whole narrative. With actual phenomena of degeneration — such as we know them from the marauding berserkers — one must, of course, also reckon.

I now turn to the individual sources.

In the election of the Halfstrekar, carried out by Stein, the grandson of the berserker Hromund, the following conditions of admission are mentioned: no one should take part who was younger than Stein — that is, eighteen years. In the courtyard stood a great stone; no one might go who could not lift it. No one might go who was not a proven man — one who was never anxious nor spoke a word of fear, nor drew back the lips of a wound in pain.

Further it is said: no one should possess a sword longer than one ell; no one should have less strength than twelve ordinary men. They were never to take women or children captive; no one should bind his wounds before the next day at the same hour. No one was to be admitted who possessed less strength and courage than had been specified. As a sign of their bravery they would never pitch their tents aboard ship nor lower the sail in a storm. (*Hálfs Saga* X.)

In Chapter X of the *Hálfs Saga* a clear distinction is made between conditions of admission and the laws governing the members of the fellowship.

From the contrast between Hjörleifr's unfortunate expedition (*Hálfs Saga* IX) and the comparison with the similar account in Saxo VII, 320 concerning the two brothers Frotho and

Haraldus — Frotho suffered only defeats because he had young married sailors with him, whereas the younger brother chose only unmarried men and always had great success — one may conclude that the Halfstrekar were unmarried. The prohibition against taking women captive also points in this direction. (The Jomsvikings likewise were unmarried.)

Similarly, the *Hrókslied* in the *Hálfs Saga* (verses 7–10) reports: No one should fear death, no one speak a word of fear, no one complain of wounds nor bind them before the next day. No one should follow a king who did not carefully observe his law. Even before eleven opponents they were not to flee. No one should harm a captive nor the wife of another man. Maidens they were to acquire for gold with the consent of the father.

Striking is the age limit among the Halfstrekar: eighteen years — Half himself is twelve years old. This is otherwise the usual age for the departure of young men. In the laws of the Jomsvikings the age limit is likewise eighteen years. This, however, is later tradition; only around the year 1000 was majority moved to the fifteenth year, among the Icelanders to the sixteenth.

In *Hrólfs Saga Kraka* 26, three trials are told of which Odin, under the name Hrane, imposes upon the heroes of Hrolf in order to select the right men for the difficult combat against Adil's sorcery and malice. Only twelve remain, with whose help Hrolf defeated Adil. These trials were as follows:

The king spent the night with his army at Hrane's dwelling. On the first night it became so cold that all, shivering from the cold, sought to cover themselves with everything available. Only Hrolf's heroes were content with the clothes they had.

On the second night Odin sent such irresistible thirst upon the men that they ran to where wine stood and drank.

On the third night Hrane had an unbearably hot fire kindled; all fled except Hrolf's heroes. At Adil's court they then had to endure yet another trial by fire.

The *Bjarkamál* also report of a great stone lying in the court at Leire which anyone who wished to join Hrolf had to lift (IV, 31).

The laws of the Jomsvikings (*Jómsvíkinga Saga* 7) are as follows: The age limit for members is eighteen to fifty years. No man shall flee before an equally strong and equally armed opponent. Each shall avenge the other like his brother. No one shall speak a word of fear nor falter in any situation.

They held property in common. No one shall utter slander against another. News was not to be made public except through the leader. No one should have a woman. Disputes were to be settled by the leader.

With all these fellowships one must, as I have already

indicated in the case of the *Hálfs Saga,* distinguish between the laws of the association and the conditions of admission.

If one looks at the requirements in the *Hálfs Saga,* one may perhaps infer from the expression that no one should join who was not a *hreystimaðr* that there were additional trials beyond the transmitted lifting of the stone. *Hreysti* means "courage and strength proven in trial."

In the Russian law of King Frode, corresponding to that of the Halfstrekar, it is said: he also decreed that whoever entered the army and claimed the reputation of tested prowess must attack one opponent, defend himself against two, retreat step by step before three, but before four might flee without shame. (Saxo V, 236; Herrmann I, p. 210.)

The men who sought admission among the Jomsvikings were likewise tested. In chapters 17 and 20 it is reported that only half of those seeking admission were found fit, while the other half were sent away again, though it is not stated what trials were imposed upon them.

The demand to endure wounds without complaint recurs in the *Hálfs Saga* and in the *Jómsvíkinga Saga* and appears entirely self-evident for the Northerners (Weinhold 315). It is conceivable that the young men were tested accordingly, just as, for example, at the court of King Harald Hardrada every soldier had to endure a blow upon the eyebrow without so much as twitching an eyelid; otherwise he was expelled from the court and dismissed (Saxo VII, 367).

A long series of conditions for admission is preserved from the Fianna.

1 No one was admitted to the great assembly, to the annual fair, or to the feast until his parents, his clan, and his relatives had given a guarantee that they would never avenge his death upon another person; consequently, he could expect to be avenged by no one but himself, and whatever harm might befall him, his friends would not on that account seek legal redress.

2 No one was admitted until he was a perfect poet and had read the twelve books of poetry.

3 No one was admitted until a wide pit had been dug for him in which he stood up to his knees, with his shield in one hand and a hazel staff the length of a warrior's arm in the other. Nine warriors, armed with nine spears, took their stand on nine ridges before him and hurled their nine spears at him simultaneously. If he was wounded despite his shield and hazel staff, he was not admitted.

4 No one was admitted until his hair had been braided and he had been driven through several forests, while the whole company of the Fianna pursued him with the full

intention of wounding him. The distance between them was only the length of a tree. If they overtook and wounded him, he was not admitted.

5 No one was admitted if the weapons in his hand trembled.

6 No one was admitted if a single braid of his hair came loose on a branch in the forest while he was being pursued.

7 No one was admitted if his foot broke a single withered twig while running.

8 No one was admitted unless he could leap over a branch at the height of his forehead or slip under a branch at knee height without slackening his speed.

9 No one was admitted unless he could pull a thorn from his heel without diminishing his speed.

10 No one was admitted without first having sworn loyalty and obedience to the king. (O'Curry II, 381 ff.)

Even after allowing for poetic exaggeration, these conditions appear possible. The first point in particular suggests that the whole institution was not a mere construction of the imagination but, cautiously expressed, at least had a real model. This provision shows that some men must have suffered serious harm in the trials. From the third point arises the rule for those admitted not to flee even before nine attackers, for every man had in fact stood his ground against nine enemies. The requirement that the disadvantaged fighter must stand in a pit, as Professor Goldmann informs me, also appears in the duel between man and woman (ordeal).

Points 4, 5, 7, 8, and 9 are pronounced tests of endurance and skill; in point 9 the complete indifference to injury plays a role. That the hair had to be so carefully braided and must not fall into disorder while running shows that the arrangement of the hair was important in this initiation. Perhaps the hair was previously worn loose for a time, as among the Chatti. Such high demands upon the candidates — even if, of course, a good deal must be discounted as exaggeration — presuppose a period of instruction in the use of weapons and in physical exercises. Is point 7 merely an exaggerated test of agility, or did the inviolate character of the forest have religious significance?

With regard to test 3 of the Fianna, one might suppose that something similar was also known in Norway, for in the *Hálfs Saga* it is said that no one should be admitted who had less strength than twelve men, and in the *Hrókslied* they would not flee even before eleven enemies. It is also conceivable that among the Jomsvikings anyone who wished to be admitted had to undergo a trial combat.

The reports discussed thus far are comparatively late and belong to one stratum of tradition. Yet much older accounts concerning the overall phenomenon have also been preserved. It underlies, for example, the structure of the fairy-tale-like narrative of Sinfjötli in the *Völsunga Saga* VII and VIII:

Signy wishes to prepare her sons for vengeance upon their father. At nine and ten years of age she tests, together with Sigmund, her own and Siggeir's sons to see whether they are fit for the task; and at their mother's counsel Sigmund slays them when they fail the trials. Again at the age of ten Sinfjötli, the son of Signy and Sigmund, is put to the test. Before sending him to Sigmund, his mother sews the sleeves to his skin, as she had done with the other two boys, so that when they were pulled off the skin came with them. The two other children could not endure it and cried out; but Sinfjötli remained silent and, when asked whether it hurt, answered: *"To a Völsung this seems but a small wound."*

Later he fearlessly kneads a poisonous serpent into the bread-dough for Sigmund. Sigmund laughs, yet thinks the boy still too young for vengeance. He wishes first to accustom him to bold deeds and endurance, and they now lead a wild life in the forest. Once they find wolf-skins (*ulfshamir*) hanging over two sleeping men; they put them on and become wolves. They agree to roam separately and to withstand seven enemies, but no more.

Sinfjötli first overcomes seven, then even eleven men alone. Thereupon Sigmund bites him in the throat, but afterwards revives him again. When they were at last able to free themselves from the wolf-skins, they burned them. And when Sinfjötli had grown to maturity, Sigmund deemed him sufficiently tested. Then follows the vengeance.

In this story a complete initiation is once narrated:

1 The boy's trial, a test of courage and steadfastness. How serious this test was is shown by what befell the other two boys.

2 The period of training in animal disguise and animal-fury, in which warfare and endurance are learned.

3 The test of manhood, the proof of standing firm against seven to eleven enemies.

The narrator no longer understands the wolf-disguise as something self-evident; he lets the wolf-garments be found by chance, put on without reason, and finally burned, as magical garments are commonly burned. The entire episode is presented in the spirit of the later belief in shapeshifting, and moreover interwoven with the fairy-tale motif of life-force. At the end it is said: during this misfortune (the wolf-life) they performed many heroic deeds in Siggeir's realm.

Especially clear here is the old intermediate period, the time of apprenticeship.

On the whole the saga still holds fairly faithfully to the old sequence: boyhood trial, receiving of weapons, a kind of apprenticeship, then the great test of manhood — usually the dragon-fight. The dragon-fight is ordinarily closely connected with winning the bride. Quite similarly runs the life of the hero in fairy-tale: first striking deed, time of apprenticeship and adventure, winning of the bride. With this the fairy-tale ends; if it continues, it usually concerns the recovery of the somehow abducted bride or wife. Precisely this typical course of the narrative indicates that it rests upon a lived reality. Certainly, one must not rely upon saga and fairy-tale alone, not least because the fairy-tale with the structure just described is very ancient, Indo-European according to Sydow, and therefore cannot serve as proof solely for early Germanic and Nordic conditions. In our case, however, it may be adduced with reference to early Germanic tradition in Tacitus.

The nature of the admission rites of the Viking bands points to a preceding period of apprenticeship; yet the bands themselves constitute a kind of probation. Noteworthy is the contradiction in the Hálf-laws between the command of celibacy on the one hand and the marriage regulations on the other. This indicates that even in these warrior-bands with military celibacy, remaining unmarried was, as among the Chatti, only temporary for part of the members.

The conception of the apprenticeship of the young man, which in the old initiation is the essential element, perhaps allows us to grasp the inner cause of the shifting of the age of majority and thus the relatively late admission age of the Viking bands.

The concept of a period of apprenticeship and probation has survived into our own time. Kaufmann (507), in the discussion of the ancient Germanic "Knappenzeit," points to the two terms of majority mentioned by Wackernagel (58): coming "to his years" and coming "to his days." Until the first point, the twelfth year, the boy must have a guardian; until the second he may have one. An echo of this remains in our present custom, that a child at fourteen acquires a limited capacity, and with majority full legal capacity.

In earlier times the age of majority was the twelfth year; yet in the North there persisted the notion that the twelve-year-old had to undertake a journey of about three years, usually entering the retinue of a king, in order thereafter to count as a full man and to be able to marry. Even in more recent times the youths, after confirmation — though admitted into the association of young men — are at first only "half-men" (*halvkar*) and may only after some years, at eighteen ("whole men," *helkarlar*), and after various tests, e.g., participation in night-visits, take full part. (Erixon 106, 109.)

This seems to be explained by the fact that approximately twelve and eighteen years were in earliest times the beginning and end points of the probationary period, the religiously significant intermediate time. When the cultic customs connected with this period disappear, the apprenticeship becomes increasingly "secular" and finally falls away as a public institution; it is then understandable that the age of majority is shifted to the earlier endpoint of the training period. The individual rites, however, migrate into already related wedding customs, into children's festivals, or become children's games, and so forth. This is a general phenomenon. Often part of the initiation rites, e.g., circumcision, is transferred into early childhood; likewise the Greek customs mentioned in the saga of Zagreus are performed upon a child.

The purpose of the associations also changes with this transformation. Originally, they had education in their hands; later their sphere of activity becomes narrower: they become explicit warrior bands. Yet every young man who wished to be regarded as fully grown had, at least temporarily, to belong to one of them.

Do the admission tests reported in the poetic tradition correspond to those of real life?

One need not be surprised at the cruelty and harshness of the conditions. Above all, a human life at that time was not valued as highly as today. I must here recall the trials of so-called "primitive" peoples, especially of North America. In all such tests the possibility had to exist that the young man would not endure them, for a selection was intended. I therefore do not believe that we must reckon with particularly great exaggeration in the tradition concerning these tests. One need only think of the harsh treatment that apprentices even today, for example among carpenters, may experience (Eugen Weiß, p. 86 ff.).

The tendency to depict the heroes of earlier times as much stronger and more capable was, of course, present. For example: Skallagrim fetched a stone from the bottom of the sea, rowed it ashore and carried it before the smithy; now (in the narrator's time) four men can no longer lift it. Naturally, the demand to stand firm against three, nine, or eleven enemies is poetic exaggeration. The law of the Jomsvikings requires only that one not flee from an equally armed opponent.

The most widespread demand placed upon a full-fledged man is battle-fury. It is expressed also in the provision of the Chatti warrior band that one must slay an enemy in order to end the probationary period. Professor Much points out that this provision cannot have been carried out strictly, for too many men would have perished; the Chatti were surrounded by enemies of equal strength.

One must reckon with a mitigation of the requirement at least for a later period. The provision remains according to its wording, but its execution is adapted to circumstances or replaced by some other achievement. Something similar has been observed among primitive peoples.

One may also compare a similar development in folk laws. In them much cruelty and impossibility is still recorded, even though it has long since ceased to be practiced, perhaps was never practiced in such severity (cf. Gierke, p. 26).

Furthermore, as Professor Much emphasises, such a provision would necessarily lead to head-hunting. Traces of this are found, for example, in *Heimskringla* 55: Jarl Sigurd tied the head of the slain Jarl Melbrigða to his saddle. Otherwise, however, it seems that the weapon taken from the enemy counted as proof of victory. Tacitus (*Germania* 31) also hints at this: *super sanguinem et spolia revelant frontem — "over blood and spoils they bare the brow."*

Taken as a whole, this demand is extraordinarily widespread and popular in our tradition, when one considers how many heroes and historical figures of the sagas begin their careers with the slaying of their father's or brother's murderer.

Almost as frequently one hears of the task of killing a wild animal. Among the Taifali it was a bear or a boar. In *Landnámabók* II, 9 it is told of Herjólfr hǫkinrazi that at the age of eight he overcame a bear that had bitten him in the buttock. The struggle of the young hero with a wild beast is a standing motif in epic poetry. As the first deed of the Icelandic hero Finnbogi a wrestling match with a bear and its killing is reported. In Saxo 1/19, Skjöldus' successful bear hunt is told as his first deed.

Unavoidably, the Grimm fairy tale of the bear-skin comes to mind here, and the conjecture seems justified that the berserkers originally had to take the bear- or wolf-skin from the animal they themselves had slain.

Besides the testimonies mentioned, which stem partly from epic and fairy-tale tradition, a very noteworthy incident is told in *Flóamannasaga* 10, which gives the impression of being drawn from life. The five-year-old Thorgils wished to take part in the games of the older boys and sought out a place where he would stand. But the other boys said that they had agreed that only he might play who had already killed a living being. Thorgils was therefore not allowed to join in. During the night the experience would not let him sleep; he rose and thrust a spear into the body of an old horse that stood at the byre, so that it fell down dead. Here we find an admission requirement, probably no longer in use among adults, imitated and preserved in a children's game.

Even in more recent folk custom (Finland), the killing of a wild animal has been preserved as a test of manhood (Holmberg, *Årsb.* 59).

Yet saga and fairy tale are not satisfied with the bear. The more lovingly the shining hero is portrayed, the more monstrous and gigantic his adversaries become (cf. Sydow, *Jättarna*, p. 44).

Thus the heroic saga replaces the native fierce animal with the foreign fabulous creature, the dragon, with which the young hero must fight.

Even outside the Viking sagas mentioned, stone-lifting is known in Old Norse literature. Of the strong Grettir (*Grettis Saga* 16) it is reported that he lifted a stone that is now called "Grettir's lift." "*Many people went there to see the stone, and it seemed to them most wondrous that so young a man was able to lift so great a boulder.*" The saga narrator no longer knows why he tells this at this point in the story and reports it merely as a curiosity. If one considers the context, however, one sees that from this moment Grettir's character changes. Until then only boyish pranks are told of him; he was a troublemaker and his strength was not precisely known (*Grettis Saga* 14). In chapter 15 Grettir is defeated in wrestling by a somewhat older boy. On his first ride to the Thing he slays a man and is declared outlawed; on the way home he lifts the stone. From then on he appears as a great hero, even though everything turns out to his misfortune.

A similar test of strength, namely the lifting of a kettle filled with sand, is reported in *Flateyjarbók* I, 524. Orm lifts it by the handle with his little finger; he was then twenty years old (cf. p. 62).

This closely related strength-test is still customary among the people (cf. Holmberg, *Årsb.* 59; Erixon, Hylén Cavallius; Andree, Braunschweig, p. 237).

Far more instructive is the ordeal by fire. It is told of Hrólf's berserkers. It is also otherwise said of berserkers that fire could not harm them, that they ran through fire. In Aðils' hall Hrólf leaps through the fire with which the king torments him and his companions, crying: *"He who shrinks from the fire fears it!"* His men follow him. To be compared with these explicit fire-ordeals is the account in *Hálfs Saga* 8, according to which Hjörleifr is suspended by his shoe-thongs between two fires. While the whole story of the faithless woman is a wandering tale (Bugge, *Forhandlinger* 40), the hanging between two fires seems to occur only in the Nordic and similarly in a German version.

A kind of fire-ordeal is also the scene in *Grímnismál* in which the king has the, admittedly suspicious, guest starve and thirst for eight days between two fires in order to force him to speak. Detter-Heinzel provide a report concerning the Lapps, according to which strangers too were tormented by fire. I believe that in both accounts we are dealing with an isolated remnant of an ancient conception: that the stranger was rightless and unprotected and therefore first had to undergo a series of initiation rites.

The torments of newcomers long persisted and for the most part have become more harmless hazings. Less harmless was the behaviour of the berserkers at the court of Frotho, which Saxo describes in Book V, 293 ff. Newcomers were pelted with gnawed bones (this is otherwise attested as well, *hnútukast*);

others forced them into excess and let them burst from immoderate drinking. A slippery hide was spread over the threshold for Ericus and, when he stepped upon it, they pulled a cord so that he would have fallen, had his brother not caught him.

A richly embellished fairy-tale account of the reception of strangers is preserved in Snorri's *Gylfaginning* 47. Thor and his companions must undergo trials upon their arrival at Útgarðaloki: contests in eating, running, drinking, lifting (cf. the stone-lifting), and wrestling. One sees how closely this narrative stands to the familiar saga reports according to which the unknown guest is, for example, challenged to a drinking contest. The final survivals of this custom are the riddle-contests with the newcomer. Similarly, the Tuscan duke Widoguerra treated minstrels. The Bolognese jurist Boncompagno recounts in his Formulary (Boncompagnus) around 1270 that he compelled one to climb a tree and fly, placed another upon the roof in snow and north wind, set one naked between two fires after smearing his body with swine's fat, and had another beaten. Importune petitioners he made stand upon a woodpile until their clothes caught fire and their beards and hair were singed (*Burdach* I, 293). In such wanton torments one must think of models effective from oral tradition or literature. One must also consider the rightlessness of medieval minstrels; they occupy a position similar to that of the guest in much earlier times.

Thus, within the treatment of guests — which in our Nordic

sources stands in complete opposition to the prescriptions of the age (cf. *Hávamál*) — ancient initiation rites are still embedded.

Thus, in the treatment of guests that is completely opposed to the prescriptions of our Nordic sources (cf. *Hávamál*), old rites of admission are still concealed.

The fire-ordeal of the berserkers does not appear improbable or unbelievable if one considers the dreadful heat that people had to endure in the numerous house-burnings (*brennur*) of the sagas. It is often told how those locked inside burning houses ran against the walls and seized burning beams as weapons (cf. Güntert 26).

Running through fire is under certain circumstances nothing extraordinary. One need only think of workers in foundries who walk barefoot over glowing slag. The foot is protected from burning by a layer of evaporating sweat droplets (spheroidal state, Wallentin 111).

But in the case of the berserkers one may recognise in the fire-ordeal a special and very ancient significance, if one casts a glance at the nature of fire-ordeals distributed across the whole world. According to Hauer (66, 371, 433), the fire-walk, the walking over glowing coals, occurs wherever capacities for ecstatic experiences are present. Among shamans too, the endurance of great heat (e.g., in the Quatabund, Melanesia), and above all the carrying of burning coals, plays an important role.

Hauer regards it decisively as a test of anaesthesia, in order to examine the strength of subconscious excitation. For a consequence of genuine ecstasy is in part insensibility to heat and cold, to stabbing and to blows. It is generally recognised that the capacity for ecstasy belongs to the essence of the berserker; the original meaning of the fire-ordeal would here likewise have been to test this capacity. If the ecstasy is not genuine, the fire-ordeal fails, as the account of Vatns clearly shows. In that the bishop consecrates the fire with the cross, the berserkers become uncertain, for to the attainment of true ecstasy belong mood and the faith of the surroundings. Often the companions of a shaman strive to bring him into ecstasy through the singing of rhythmic songs. Exactly the same is told in *Örvar-Odds Saga* II. The völva Heiðr has fifteen young men and fifteen maidens with her who must sing songs in order to support her in her magic. In *Vatnsdœla Saga,* precisely the opposite is achieved through the blessing of the bishop.

Now the expression *hvárki flýja eld né járn — "to flee neither fire nor iron"* (*Hrólfs Saga Kraka,* ch. 33; 28; *Völsunga Saga* 5) — gains a particular meaning. The berserkers must originally have undergone the test implied by this phrase. In the cited passages, however, it is now only said that the heroes in their youth swore to flee neither fire nor iron. Yet in view of the assertion that neither fire nor iron could harm the berserker, one may assume for the older period a trial of this kind such as is handed down for Hrólfr's berserkers.

The fire-ordeal has undergone a transformation in the consciousness of the old Norsemen, as was already indicated in the first chapter. The originally religious — that is, the testing of ecstatic disposition — became a test of courage and steadfastness. What earlier was practiced for cultic and probably also martial purposes later serves merely martial training without religious significance.

A degeneration into mere showmanship also seems to have occurred; the sword-swallowing berserkers (Saxo 326, 328) recall the fire-eaters of our fairs.

Very often it is told in the sagas that the berserkers could blunt weapons with their gaze. Perhaps this idea belongs, in essence, on the same level as the story of the shirts that make one invulnerable. The warrior who is in himself invulnerable is no longer common; the cause of invulnerability is shifted to a magical act. Güntert (18) draws attention to the fact that Odin boasts in *Hávamál* 148 (according to Bugge): *"The blade I make blunt for my enemies."* Thus once again a new connection between Odin and the berserkers. Invulnerability to iron is also understood as a gift of Odin to his favourite: *"Odin granted Framar that no iron wounded him."* (*Saga Ketils Hængs*, p. 132.)

Chapter 6 of the *Ynglinga Saga* likewise expresses the intimate connection of Odin with the raging berserkers, as I have already indicated.

1 The berserkers are equated with Odin's (the leader of the host of the dead) men of the dead host.

2 In their ecstasy they stand especially close to the god of ecstasy.

Both characteristics are already expressed in the name of the god. Much takes the basic meaning of *wod* in the name Wodan to be "moving air"; from this his character as storm-god and leader of the host of the dead is to be understood. Much also agrees with Klage's interpretation, who relates the name to Old Norse *óþr* "poem," Anglo-Saxon *wōþ* "song, chant," Latin *vates* "inspired singer," Irish *faith* "poet," with the basic meaning: vehement stirring of the soul; though Much considers this to be a derived meaning. Perhaps it is also not accidental that precisely Odin imposes the trials upon Hrolf's berserkers.

But how is the later insertion of the scene into the *Hrólfs Saga Kraka* to be understood? The final redactor of the story, who gave it the form known to us, must have been a genuine saga-man, who inserted ancient inherited motifs at the psychologically appropriate point in his narrative. This is a process one can observe very often. If A. Olrik speaks of the poetic gravity of certain conceptions around which, as it were, floating tradition gathers, then there are likewise psychological focal points in the course of a narrative, places where old symbols and old traditions press to the surface; these are above all the important transitional and preparatory periods.

With this in mind, the heightened portrayal (p. 66) of the berserkers' conduct at Frotho's court in Saxo becomes intelligible (V. 188). One must first consider the overall situation. The retinue grows wild during the three years of peace, and conditions are presented by Saxo as particularly desolate so that the order that soon follows may appear all the more impressive and the king, after his inglorious and softened youth, may stand forth all the more splendidly. To this general situation, which is to be characterised, we owe the description of the habits of the berserkers, from which Frotho's laws turn away.

All the individual details communicated, however, are initiation rites; part of them is already known from the discussed conditions of admission. The passage runs, according to Herrmann's translation:

"They hoisted some up by ropes into the air and tormented them in such a way that they let them swing up and down like a ball; others they made step onto a goatskin and, if they were not attentive, brought them down upon the slippery hide by a pull on a hidden rope; others they stripped of their clothes and tore them with blows of whips; others they fastened to clubs and carried out a mock hanging as if by a noose; others singed beard and hair with burning splinters of pine; others burned their private parts with a firebrand held beneath. They did not allow maidens to marry until they had sacrificed their chastity to them. The strangers pelted them with bones; others forced them to excess and let them burst from immoderate drinking. No one was permitted to

marry off his daughter unless he had first purchased their favour and goodwill. No one might take a wife unless he had first dearly bought her consent."

All this sounds thoroughly archaic. The conduct toward the maidens I have discussed above (p. 65). The singeing and burning correspond to the fire ordeal. Very significant is the twice-mentioned hanging; the second time it is explicitly a mock hanging (gallows).

Hjǫrleifr too was hanged. If one thinks of the mock sacrifice which, according to the account of Vikarr (*Gautreks Saga* 7), was to be performed, the meaning of hanging originally appears to be a sacrificial rite to Odin, as indeed those who are hanged belong to Odin (*hangadrottinn*, "lord of the hanged"). One might still doubt whether mock hanging was an initiation rite of the bands. If one does not wish to accept Saxo's account as proof, one must turn to considerably later evidence.

At the deposition, as the *Manuale scholarium* of 1480 reports (Jarncke, chap. II), the novice was hung on a rope. The same initiation custom existed in the trading house of the German Hanse in Bergen. The novice was bound to a rope, drawn up into the air and at the same time smoked, then whipped until blood flowed and furthermore pressed onto a hide (Holberg II, 59). These games are admittedly only transmitted from the seventeenth century, but their antiquity can no longer be doubted. It is possible that Nordic tradition also plays a part in them; doubtless old German rites, most of which survive as games (Hartung).

The placing of smooth hides in order to bring someone to a fall is also mentioned in *Egils Saga* 28; thereby one berserker falls and can be slain.

Particularly noteworthy is that newcomers are forced into excessive drinking; this recalls the drinking customs of students.

One sees that these are by no means senseless inventions of Saxo; rather, he presents a series of inherited initiation customs as an outgrowth of the unrestrained and idle nature of the berserkers.

One sees that these are by no means senseless inventions of Saxo; rather, he presents a series of transmitted initiation customs as an outgrowth of the unrestrained and idle behaviour of the berserkers.

In all the customs discussed, the close relationship between initiation rites and punishments is striking. This may be explained by the fact that the leagues and later the young men's associations held penal authority in their hands, as has been preserved especially for penalties of honour and morality in rural districts down to our own time (cf. Haberlandt, *Hochzeitsbrauch* 5). In the mock hanging and mock burning, a connection with the old public death penalties — hanging and burning for sacrificial purposes (Amira 198, 219) — is evident. The remaining admission customs seem, in later times, when their original meaning had faded, to have been understood and practiced as punishments; in part they live on as games. Thus, for example, the "pressing" at the initiation of the butchers and as a baker's punishment is customary and survives further as a children's game.

It has been shown that all the individual elements of the reports from which we proceeded are widely disseminated, both in literature and in later folk custom. Thus the laws and initiation rites of the legendary leagues also allow conclusions about real conditions, and in them, according to these attestations, one will recognise remnants of ancient *männerbünde* and initiations of youths.

In broad outlines, one may imagine the development reflected in the literary sources discussed as follows.

Initiation and the cultic leagues reach back into Indo-Germanic times. Schröder has shown that even the representation of the host of the dead by the young men's association is an Indo-Germanic custom. Clear traces in folktales and totemistic features prove the great antiquity. The relationship to Wodan, which stands out so clearly in our sources, is significantly younger. It has been repeatedly emphasised that initiation already assumed a distinctly warlike significance in ancient Germanic times. This transformation

III

Layers of the Tradition

In the preceding section I attempted, on the basis of the preserved written tradition, to sketch a picture of the ancient Germanic men's leagues and the initiation of youths; yet some further clarification and additions are still necessary.

Taken as a whole, I would like to distinguish three clearly recognisable layers within the tradition.

1 A very old Indo-Germanic, perhaps even pre-Indo-Germanic layer. For understanding this oldest foundation, comparison with the initiations of so-called primitive cultures was indispensable. At this level, ecstatic experience forms the central core of religion as such. Representation and the represented, religious experience and religious action, coincide completely. When speaking of the experiences of this stage, one must exclude the concept of "fantasy" in the usual sense, since here, as in childhood, no distinction is yet made between imagination and reality (Spranger 32; Lévy-Bruhl 50,

338). The barely discernible traces of this unified, undivided experience can be followed down into the tradition of a very late period.

To be sure, one had to proceed somewhat one-sidedly in doing so. I have already pointed this out in discussing the word group *hamast–hamr*, and it was unavoidable, when treating this oldest layer, to work repeatedly with concepts of a much later time. A clear separation between the old conception and later beliefs about the soul (in which the soul is still imagined in bodily form) was not possible. This is particularly evident in the almost no longer graspable connection between berserkers and the *einherjar*, or in the merging of berserker and werewolf myths.

From this layer derive the distinctly totemistic features. The wide distribution of the various ordeals indicates that they too belong to this oldest stage.

For the purposes of this study, however, the further development and transformation of the institution in the ancient Germanic period is of primary importance. If comparison with primitive cultures could clarify much for the earliest period, this developmental stage must above all be understood from within ancient Germanic culture itself.

The difficulties and sources of error for this second layer are considerable. The possibilities of religious experience are more differentiated and refined; interpretations, reflections, artistic reshaping, and imaginative elaboration — even of individual elements — affect the oral tradition, and even more so the written one.

Viewed as a whole, the southern and northern Germanic sources yield, in their main outlines, a unified picture: the leagues still possess recognisable religious significance; they hold the education and training of the youth in their hands and stand in the service of military leadership.

For the South we depend on a few brief reports of foreign historians (1st-8th century A.D.). In the North the written tradition is much richer, but also later (12th-14th century), so that one cannot expect from it an entirely faithful or immediately comprehensible picture of the old institution.

Although it has been shown that all the details of this tradition are widely distributed in both older and later times, judging from what we otherwise know about initiation and from more recent folk custom, one gains the impression that only part of the overall phenomenon has been preserved.

For this reason I would distinguish, within the total Nordic tradition concerning our subject, two layers:

1 A literary (bookish) tradition — the Viking saga tradition — in which the leagues enter into close association with Odin, who, as leader of the dead, as god of ecstasy, and

as god of the noble and warrior classes, embodies all the fundamental traits of the old leagues;

2 Alongside this, one must reckon with a popular further development of the old foundational layer, belonging to the unwritten, more peasant tradition. It stands in uninterrupted connection with the other, even though the latter has undergone a particular development of its own. From it the literary tradition continually receives new impulses; this becomes tangible, for example, in the conduct of the berserkers and the Fianna toward women.

The fact that the berserkers held processions, perhaps even performed dances, and that masks were used — bear, wolf, and dog masks have been identified — points beyond the strictly Viking literary tradition and toward later folk customs.

While Odin, who in North as in South appears connected with the leagues, was in the North the god of the upper class — in contrast to the peasant god Thor — in Germany he appears as a wind god in closest relation to fertility and harvest blessing. This has survived most clearly in his association with the Wild Hunt. In Mecklenburg, until recent times, a sheaf of ears of grain was left standing in his honour in the field.

If the Wild Hunt and its representation by the youth bands — whose dances must in part be interpreted as vegetation magic — are meant to bring fertility, then the connection between initiation of youths and fertility magic is entirely consistent with primitive initiation. The magical connection between human and animal-plant fertility repeatedly emerges in folk customs. Particularly suited to such analogical magic are young people in the first bloom of life, who in these rites at the same time receive consecration for their own fertility.

Equally important is the idea that the dead — usually the ancestors, whom the youths represent — exercise influence over the growth of plants (Schröder 477). Among primitive peoples these connections are represented through dances and through the central theme of initiation: death and rebirth of the one being initiated.

While nothing of this is heard in the Viking tradition, a custom described by Tacitus (*Germania* 24) falls within this same circle of ideas: the sword-dance.

The sword-dance has already been examined thoroughly and in detail, especially by Müllenhoff. But only Schröder explicitly connects it with the initiation of youths. Tacitus tells of a dangerous weapon-dance. Yet not only in later folk tradition has a small drama been preserved that is performed during the sword-dance, in which one is apparently slain and then revived; something very similar is also reported of the sword-dance of the Thracians (Xenophon, *Anabasis* VI, 1, 5): *"The Thracians performed the dance to the flute, making high leaps with agility, swinging and clashing their swords against one another; at last one rushed upon the other, the one struck fell as if dead; the victor stripped him of his armour and departed singing the song of triumph, while the fallen man was carried away."* (Naumann 134.)

For the North an early testimony to the sword-dance is lacking, unless one wishes to regard the so-called "Gothic" Yule-play as such.

Müllenhoff assumes that, although no literary testimony has survived, the sword-dance in the North is likewise ancient. He is also of the opinion that killing and reviving belong to the very core of the dance. That precisely this fits into the circle of initiation rites needs no further emphasis.

One must therefore reckon, with Müllenhoff, with a very ancient tradition that has accidentally not entered into literature. Nevertheless, the question must be raised whether traces of a rebirth rite have not in fact been preserved, even if in altered and difficult-to-recognise form.

This question, as well as the reason why in later folk tradition agricultural customs play such a prominent role in rites of consecration, still requires investigation.

For the greater part of the initiation rites it has been shown that they stem from very ancient times and were already practiced by the old Germanic peoples.

Initiation Rites of Young Men and Male Warrior Brotherhoods in Early Germanic Culture

A Contribution to the Study of Germanic and Nordic Antiquity and Folklore

Was written by Dr. Lily Weiser
and translated into English by Tom Billinge.

Learn more about Tom at **TomBillinge.com**.

If you enjoyed this book, consider reading *The Aryan Männerbund* by Stig Wikander and *The Feast of Immortality* by Georges Dumézil, both translated by Tom Billinge.

Watch for future translations by Tom from Sanctus Arya Press.

EX UMBRA IN SOLEM

From the translator of this book...

HEROES OF GREEK MYTH

Written by Tom Billinge

The ***Heroes of Greek Myth*** series explores the heroic archetypes and metaphysical lessons taught in the mythology of Ancient Greece. Spanning several generations of heroes, Tom Billinge examines the timeless truths handed down to us through the millennia.

Undying Glory: The Solar Path of Greek Heroes is the first of Billinge's books. More than just a recounting of the tales of Greek heroes, it is a blueprint for modern to men to follow. The work focuses on six heroes in particular as they traverse the Solar Path, each aiming to become Solar Man – a state above the gods.

Age of Heroes: Beyond the Solar Path lays out a framework of the Ancient Greek Heroic Age as a model for a return to the values of that time. It analyzes concepts that can be gleaned from the *Iliad* and *Odyssey*, placing them in their original context within the complete *Epic Cycle*. With esoteric lessons drawn out from the Homeric material, this is a manual for the modern-day heroic aspirant looking to reach greatness.

Return to Hyperborea: The Heroic Initiate culminates the trilogy, postulating the hero Orpheus as transmitter of ancient Hyperborean mysteries to the Hellenic people. Looking at the Indo-European Wolf Cult in the context of Ancient Greece, this final installment in the series delves into the mystery traditions of both Samothaki and Eleusis before piecing together a Hyperborean initiatic lineage handed down through Orphic mystery rites and theogonic material.

The highly acclaimed ***Heroes of Greek Myth*** series is a triumphant call for a resurgence of true heroism in a time that so critically needs it.

Pickup your copies now at major booksellers.

Tom at the Sanctuary of the Great Gods in Samothrace, Greece

About the Translator

Tom Billinge is originally from England and lives in the USA. He grew up surrounded by Ancient Greek mythology, culture, archaeology and history, as his father was a historical geographer and his mother was Greek. After graduating with a degree in archaeology, Tom moved to Asia, where he explored temples and immersed himself in the martial and spiritual traditions of the East.

Following several years travelling the world and writing for a living, Tom returned to the West and to his roots. This led to his first book, *Undying Glory: The Solar Path of Greek Heroes* that examines the first heroes of Greek mythology. Tom then continued the series with an exploration of the Homeric material in *Age of Heroes: Beyond the Solar Path*. The final book of the trilogy, *Return to Hyperborea: The Heroic Initiate*, examines the Orphic tradition.

With a particular interest in Indo-European matters, Tom spends much of his time making connections between the spiritual and martial impulses of the various Indo-European cultures. His book *WarYoga* explores the Indic branch of the Indo-European physical alchemical practice, while the sequel, *WarYoga: Zurxāne* deals with the Iranian tradition. The third part, *WarYoga: Palaistra,* was released in 2025. These works are the culmination of years of academic, spiritual, and physical research.

Tom has also translated several works including the Iranian epic *Garšaspname, The Aryan Männerbund* by Stig Wikander, and *The Feast of Immortality* by Georges Dumézil. *Varuna-Ouranos* by Georges Dumézil, *Pythagoras and Orpheus* by Karl Kerényi, and *Theophania* by Walter Otto are slated for future release by Sanctus Arya Press.

In addition to authoring books, articles, and essays, he teaches Muay Thai, Jiu Jitsu, Old English bareknuckle, Ancient Greek Pankrátion, and works as an editor in combat sports media. Tom is a Fellow of the Royal Asiatic Society.

For more information about Tom Billinge and his work, visit his website at **TomBillinge.com**.

www.ingramcontent.com/pod-product-compliance
Lightning Source LLC
LaVergne TN
LVHW010923110826
845149LV00013B/2457

* 9 7 8 1 9 6 8 3 9 4 0 6 6 *